UNDERWATER PHOTOGRAPHER
DAVID DOUBILET

ROLEX GLIDELOCK
EXTENSION SYSTEM

CALIBRE 3230

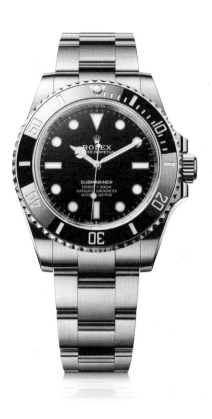

OYSTER PERPETUAL SUBMARINER

ROLEX

PARACHUTE

All the feels.

TF Design
Modern Designs in Resin

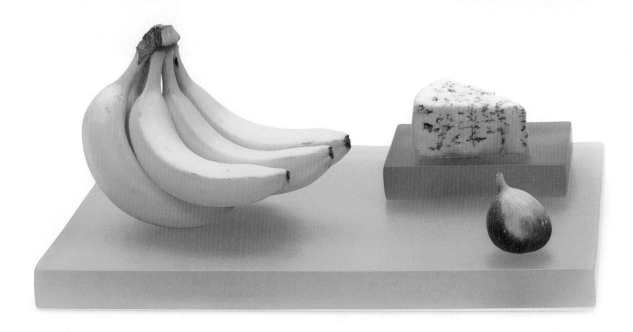

KINFOLK

MAGAZINE	EDITOR-IN-CHIEF	John Clifford Burns
	EDITOR	Harriet Fitch Little
	ART DIRECTOR	Christian Møller Andersen
	DESIGN DIRECTOR	Alex Hunting
	COPY EDITOR	Rachel Holzman
	FACT CHECKER	Gabriele Dellisanti
	DESIGN INTERN	Bethany Rush
STUDIO	ADVERTISING DIRECTOR	Edward Mannering
	SALES & DISTRIBUTION DIRECTOR	Edward Mannering
	STUDIO & PROJECT MANAGER	Susanne Buch Petersen
	DESIGNER & ART DIRECTOR	Staffan Sundström
	DIGITAL MANAGER	Cecilie Jegsen
	CO-FOUNDER	Nathan Williams

STYLING, HAIR & MAKEUP

Dominick Barcelona, Dana Boyer, Gabriela Cobar, Michelle Dacillo, Lianna Fowler, Andreas Frienholt, Dennis Gots, Jaiver Irigoyen, Tomihiro Kono, Katy Lassen, Hyunwoo Lee, Katie Mellinger, Mike O'Gorman, Seongseok Oh, Riona O'Sullivan, Rebecca Ramsey, Tomi Roppongi, Naoko Saita, Natasha Severino, Sandy Suffield, Kingsley Tao, Yeon You

WORDS

Fedora Abu, Alex Anderson, Katie Calautti, Stephanie d'Arc Taylor, Cody Delistraty, Gabriele Dellisanti, Daphnée Denis, Andrew Durbin, Tom Faber, Deborah Feldman, Alia Gilbert, Bella Gladman, Margaret Hagan, Harry Harris, Tim Hornyak, Robert Ito, Rebecca Liu, Stevie Mackenzie-Smith, Kyla Marshell, Megan Nolan, Okechukwu Nzelu, Hettie O'Brien, Kursat Ozenc, Stephanie Phillips, Debika Ray, Asher Ross, Peter Smisek, Selena Takigawa Hoy, Annick Weber

ART & PHOTOGRAPHY

Yumna Al-Arashi, Gustav Almestål, Louis Barthélemy, Matteo Bianchessi, Jo Ann Callis, Valerie Chiang, Giseok Cho, Justin Chung, Ignacio Cobo, Pelle Crépin, Laura Emerson, Kata Geibl, Gabriel Isak, Kanya Iwana, Cecilie Jegsen, Ruth Kaplan, Annie Lai, Ricardo Leite, Salva Lopez, Sayaka Maruyama, Dóra Maurer, Katie McCurdy, László Moholy-Nagy, Emman Montalvan, William Mortensen, Christian Møller Andersen, Elizaveta Porodina, Rahi Rezvani, Paul Rousteau, Tekla Evelina Severin, Patricia Sofra, Dominik Tarabanski, Aaron Tilley

CROSSWORD	Anna Gundlach
PUBLICATION DESIGN	Alex Hunting Studio
COVER PHOTOGRAPH	Giseok Cho

Kinfolk (ISSN 2596-6154) is published quarterly by Ouur ApS, Amagertorv 14, 1, 1160 Copenhagen, Denmark. Printed by Park Communications Ltd in London, United Kingdom. Color reproduction by Park Communications Ltd in London, United Kingdom. All rights reserved. No part of this publication may be reproduced, distributed or transmitted in any form or by any means, including photocopying or other electronic or mechanical methods, without prior written permission of the editor in chief, except in the case of brief quotations embodied in critical reviews and certain other noncommercial uses permitted by copyright law. The US annual subscription price is $87 USD. Airfreight and mailing in the USA by WN Shipping USA, 156-15, 146th Avenue, 2nd Floor, Jamaica, NY 11434, USA. Application to mail at periodicals postage prices is pending at Jamaica NY 11431. US Postmaster: Send address changes to Kinfolk, WN Shipping USA, 156-15, 146th Avenue, 2nd Floor, Jamaica, NY 11434, USA. Subscription records are maintained at Ouur ApS, Amagertorv 14, 1, 1160 Copenhagen, Denmark. *info@kinfolk.com, www.kinfolk.com*. Published by Ouur ApS, Amagertorv 14, Level 1, 1160 Copenhagen, Denmark. The views expressed in Kinfolk magazine are those of the respective contributors and are not necessarily shared by the company or its staff. SUBSCRIBE *Kinfolk* is published four times a year. To subscribe, visit *www.kinfolk.com/subscribe* or email us at *info@kinfolk.com*. CONTACT US If you have questions or comments, please write to us at *info@kinfolk.com*. For advertising and partnership inquiries, get in touch at *advertising@kinfolk.com*.

The Kinfolk Garden

HOW *to* LIVE WITH NATURE

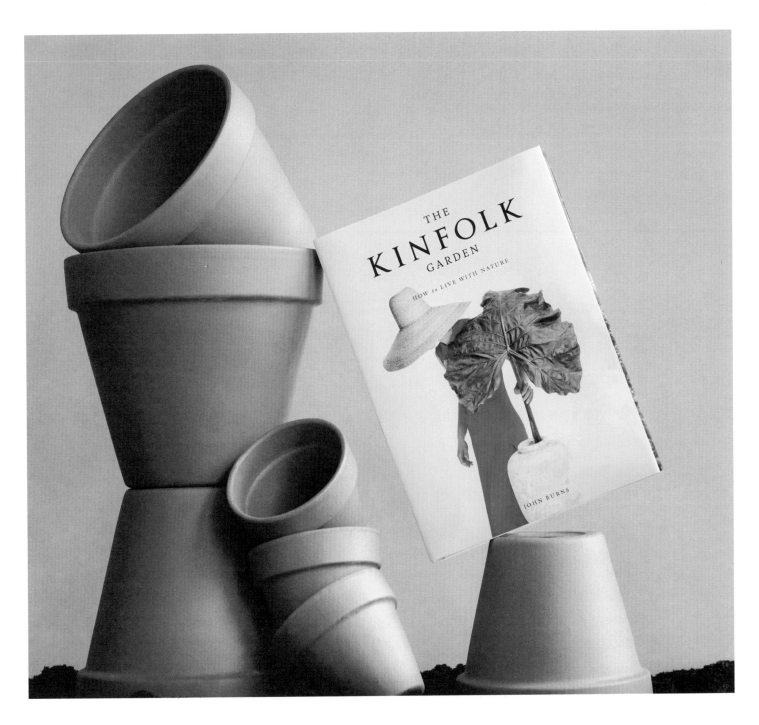

Anchored around a belief in nature as nourishment, *The Kinfolk Garden* offers simple ideas for bringing nature home. With a focus on spaces that bring the outdoors in and the indoors out, the team behind *Kinfolk* magazine explores lush gardens and plant-filled homes around the world while introducing the inspiring people who coax them into bloom.

PUBLISHED BY ARTISAN

Now available to order via kinfolk.com/shop

Starters

Features

14 – 44

46 – 112

"I'd rather fully embody the darkness in my art so I don't do it in my life."

MIRANDA JULY – P. 57

Photograph: Emman Montalvan

CONTENTS

Rituals

Directory

114 – 176

178 – 192

"Rituals are a way that we can create a sense of wholeness, peace and understanding."

NATALIA ROSENBAUM – P. 176

Photograph: Giseok Cho

håndværk

A specialist label creating *luxury basics.*
Ethically crafted with an unwavering
commitment to *exceptional quality.*

handvaerk.com

On opening this issue of *Kinfolk*, you may well be reflecting on a personal ritual you hold dear: a morning meditation, coffee drunk in a favorite spot, or perhaps a complicated beauty regimen. Without wishing to imply that these moments are *not* rituals (turn to page 169 for a full definition), they're not the focus of this issue. Instead, we explore rituals as they relate to community: the acts that bind us to each other and mark our transition from one life stage to the next. Understood in this light, it is hard for rituals to be "personal" because it is through repetition and shared understanding that they acquire meaning.

The binding role of ritual was felt particularly acutely by Abby Stein, who occupies the unique position of being the first openly transgender woman to have left Williamsburg's Hasidic community. On page 124, she speaks to *Unorthodox* author Deborah Feldman about how tradition was used within the community to limit individual freedoms. Now, eight years after her departure, she is making a cautious return to the aspects of ritual she holds dear through her work as a rabbi. "I started missing the fun part," she says. Elsewhere, on page 146, Kyla Marshell interviews death doula Alua Arthur, whose mission is to create a more meaningful engagement with life's final ritual, which many of us are too fearful to prepare for. "Talking about your death won't make it come," she says. "It's already coming."

One realization we had while researching this issue was that many of life's small milestones currently pass without ceremony. In a collaboration with Silicon Valley's Ritual Design Lab, we set out to change this by creating six new rituals that bring small moments of gravitas to common occurrences, including new etiquette for how to mourn the death of a houseplant, how to lure a lost handbag back and how to make resolutions while traveling using only an inflatable pillow.

And, after six months of limited travel themselves, our contributors were happy to have the opportunity to get back in the studio. Turn to page 46 to see our feature interview with artist and filmmaker Miranda July, which saw a full team back in a Los Angeles studio for the first time since lockdown began. The constraints imposed earlier this year fueled a lot of creativity, and we've tried to make sure the good bits endure. On page 70, for example, you'll see a story told through a series of Egyptian *khayamiya* tapestries, commissioned especially for *Kinfolk*.

JOHN CLIFFORD BURNS & HARRIET FITCH LITTLE

PORTUGUESE
KNOWLEDGE
Flannel
IN A
NEW WORLD

WWW.PORTUGUESEFLANNEL.COM

1.

Starters

14 — 44

Lost Grandeur

What happened to the wonders of the world?

Martin Parker, a professor of organization studies at the University of Bristol, offered a vision for the future of human progress in an essay for *Aeon* earlier this year: "In the hands of technology entrepreneurs... the future has been displaced into the soma of fantasy, colonised by people who want you to pay a subscription for an app. This is a future of sorts, but it's a business school version in which everything is pretty much the same, just a bit smarter and more profitable."

The original seven wonders of the world, as described by the Greek poet Antipater of Sidon, only existed simultaneously for about 60 years, the time between when the Colossus of Rhodes was completed in around 280 B.C. and when it was destroyed by an earthquake in 226 B.C. Yet the reputation of these great towering structures, unrivaled in scale and in artistry, lives on.

At the turn of the millennium, a Swiss-born Canadian filmmaker named Bernard Weber began a campaign to designate seven *new* wonders of the world. Of the 20 candidates, only two came from the 20th century: the Sydney Opera House, built in 1959, and Rio de Janeiro's Christ the Redeemer statue, finished in 1931. The other 18 were ancient: the Taj Mahal, the Great Wall of China. Even the Statue of Liberty was more than a century old at that point. Why was so little from the 20th century capable of conjuring wonder?

When we think of awe, we think of something that challenges our conception of the world. It is a grounding feeling. To drive across the Golden Gate Bridge, see the Hoover Dam, or look at the Eiffel Tower standing tall in the center of Paris reminds us of the puny scale of our individual endeavors. These experiences of enormity are essentially democratic. They are huge enough that they can be seen by all, and are intended for public use or utility.

There has been no letup in our desire to push the limits of engineering and architecture—after all, of the 50 tallest buildings in the world today, only six were built pre-2000. And yet, these modern skyscrapers don't inspire the same kind of reverence. They may be impressive, imposing structures, but at their core they are temples of finance and wealth, often emblematic of a stratum of society that many of us will never see.

What could elicit the same feelings that Antipater of Sidon had centuries ago? Where are the projects whose reputations could endure through word alone? Ironically, the great wonders of the modern world will likely be built by people working on things we can't see at all: physicists who smash subatomic particles together looking for something dubbed the "God particle"; researchers in laboratories working on vaccines to stop the next global pandemic; people theorizing on the steps we need to take to avoid climate catastrophe. These are intangible things that will challenge our conception of the world, and the direction the world is going. Things that can't be seen, but whose wonder will be felt by everyone.

Words by Harry Harris

The Comfort Zone

Don't gain, maintain.

In her 2019 book, *How to Do Nothing: Resisting the Attention Economy*, artist and writer Jenny Odell rails against the need for continual achievement. "In the context of health and ecology, things that grow unchecked are often considered parasitic or cancerous," she writes. "Yet we inhabit a culture that privileges novelty and growth over the cyclical and the regenerative." In Western societies today, Odell argues, people are too quick to believe that "new" is inherently good. [1]

There's a gendered aspect to this dichotomy, reflected in how we see traditional female and male roles. The unglamorous practice of maintenance is the domain of women: Repetitive activities such as childrearing, housekeeping, cleaning and caregiving are all demeaned and underpaid, if paid at all, as well as being viewed as unskilled. Meanwhile, men dominate the sphere of action and movement—building, fighting, inventing and exploring.

This hunger for the new has very literally shaped the world we live in—urban development, for example, celebrates the process of tearing down and building up again. Meanwhile, the urgent need to curb construction and refurbish existing buildings for the sake of the planet continues to be a secondary concern in the creation of our cities. "There still isn't really a vocabulary or an ease in discussing maintenance, since it's not really the sexiest topic," explains Hilary Sample, co-founder of US-based practice MOS Architects and author of the book *Maintenance Architecture* (2016). "But the reality is everything ages and requires upkeep."

Maintenance is worthwhile not just for practical and environmental reasons, but also for social ones, Sample says. "If those maintaining a building were to have more prominent spaces within it, that would radically change the users' relationship to the community within it, and would create a sense of sharing," she says. The simple act of asking how to keep something clean, rather than wondering who will clean it up later can create a greater interest in how a system lasts, she believes. In other words, collaborative preservation is a core element of community.

We are living at a time when the problems of privileging growth above all else are impossible to ignore: In the summer of 2020, when the world came to a standstill, GDP—the pulse of the world economy—plummeted. It has since become clear that when we're not shopping, eating, producing, traveling and accomplishing, the foundations of our economic model start to crumble, leaving governments torn between trying to save lives and restarting the engines of consumption.

Against this backdrop it has also become apparent that it is the maintainers—the caregivers, the suppliers of food and medicines, those keeping our utilities and technology functioning—who really sustain us. [2] When normality returns, will we remember a time when frequently cleaned public bathrooms felt like the most important thing of all?

Words by Debika Ray

NOTES

1. Odell cites the work of Mierle Laderman Ukeles as an example of how some artists are trying to change the way we think about maintenance work. For *Touch Sanitation Performance* (1979-1980), she spent 11 months shaking hands with every one of New York's 8,500 sanitation workers.
—
—

2. During the global pandemic of COVID-19, British key workers (such as healthcare and emergency service workers, but also cleaners, waste collectors and postal workers) were all shown appreciation through the initiative Clap for Our Carers, in which the British public gave a round of applause outside their homes each Thursday evening. Millions are reported to have taken part.

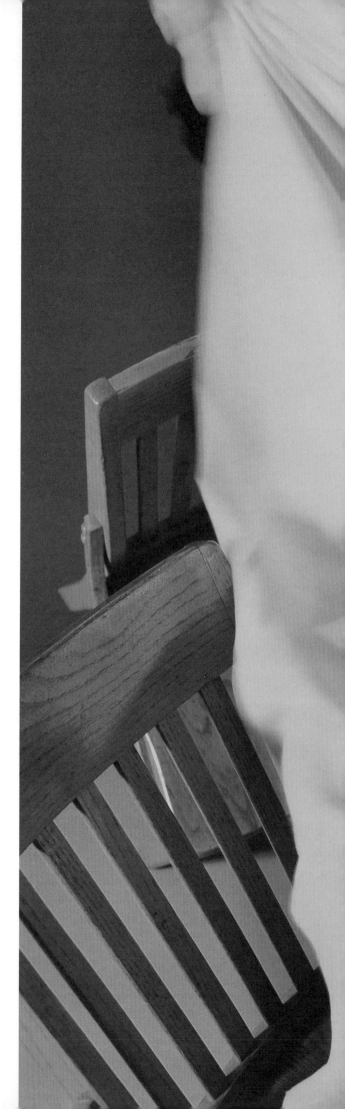

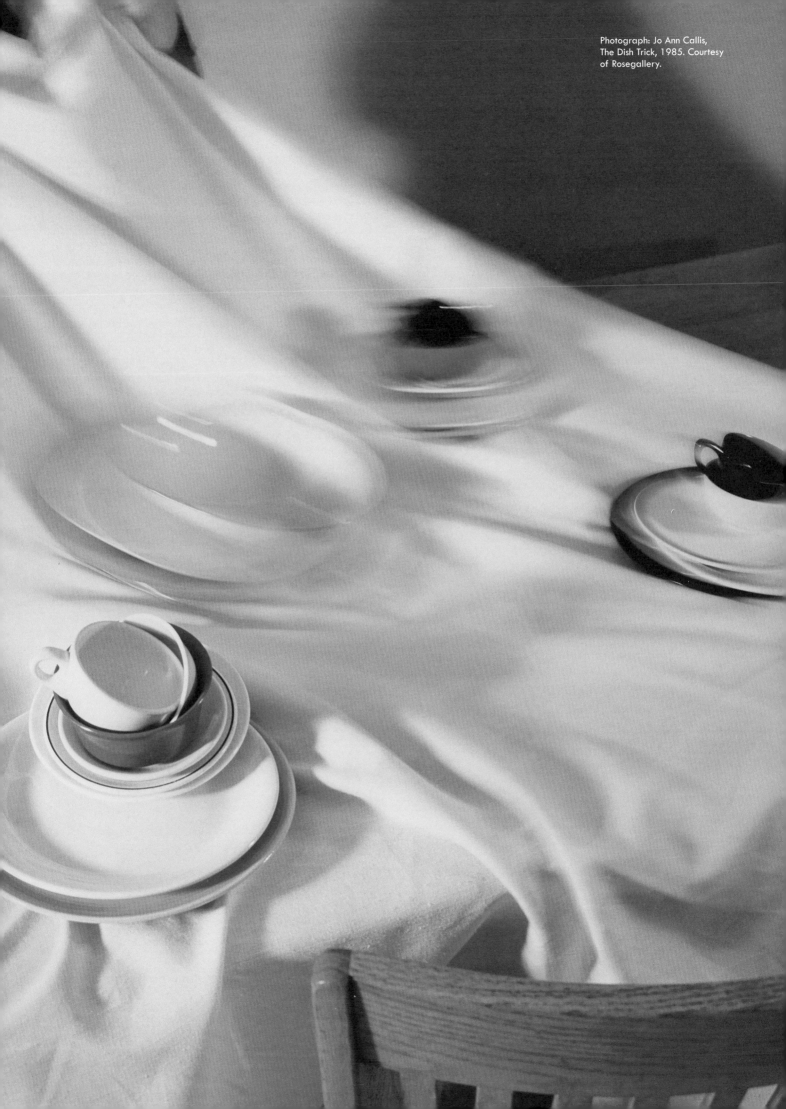

FOXFIRE

by John Clifford Burns

In 1966, Eliot Wigginton, a teacher in Rabun Gap, Georgia, set his high-school students an oral-history assignment: Go home and talk—*really talk*—to their relatives. From those conversations came stories of traditions and rituals still thriving in the region: hog dressing, log cabin building, mountain crafts, snake lore, faith healing and moonshining. In an attempt to make his classes more fun, Wigginton and his students turned the stories into *Foxfire*—a magazine and, eventually, a 12-volume anthology of southern Appalachian heritage (named after the region's glow-in-the-dark fungus). Over half a century later, the series' philosophy of self-sufficiency and simple living has renewed relevance. In the introduction of the first volume, Wigginton wrote presciently: "They have something to tell us about self-reliance, human interdependence, and the human spirit that we would do well to listen to."

Very Superstitious

Why even the most logical minds yield to magical thinking.

You may be surprised to learn that behind closed doors, lots of people are knocking on wood, holding their breath when driving past graveyards, or avoiding crossing paths with black cats. In one YouGov poll, only 13% of respondents claimed to be superstitious—but almost three times that many believed that finding a penny brings good luck. Superstition inveigles itself on even the most logical minds: According to research published in *Nature*, many scientists watch their experiments obsessively in the hope of encouraging positive results.

It's a tough habit to kick because it appeals in those moments when the stakes are highest. We need the help of this horseshoe, or that four-leaf clover, or this rabbit's foot because so often we feel helpless without them. At crucial moments, blowing on dice or crossing our fingers makes us feel like we have some control in a world where we are powerless. But no wonder so many of us are quick to disavow such beliefs: They humble us. Giving into luck means giving in to the idea that the world can turn on a dime. A missed glance over a toast can have repercussions that last seven years. Or, looked at another way, a meeting of eyes at the right moment can bring fruitful results.

Superstition is the rickety bridge over the chasm at the end of a chase: it is both risk and remedy. The poet Alice Fulton explores superstition in "The Fortunes of Aunt Fran," in which Fran "...bobs through/ my mind like a dingy, riding out/ jinxes, ill winds, and tidal waves." Long after her aunt's death, Fulton carries with her the memory of Fran's view that the world is partly knowable, partly magical. Whatever the empirical truth of things may be, Fran's beliefs offer a kind of magic in themselves.

Considered in this light, it is not surprising that superstition has such a strong hold on the human psyche. If we can take the good with the bad, the variety it offers is part of the fun.
Words by Okechukwu Nzelu

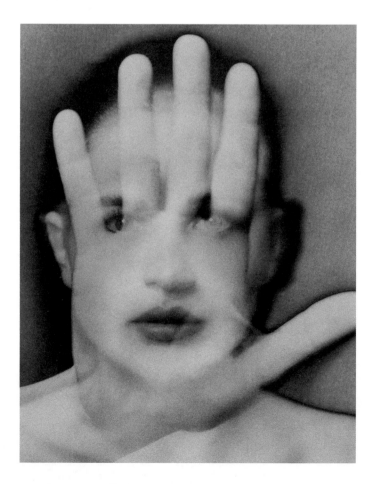

Photograph: László and Lucia by László Moholy-Nagy. Courtesy of Stiftung Bauhaus Dessau / Image by Google

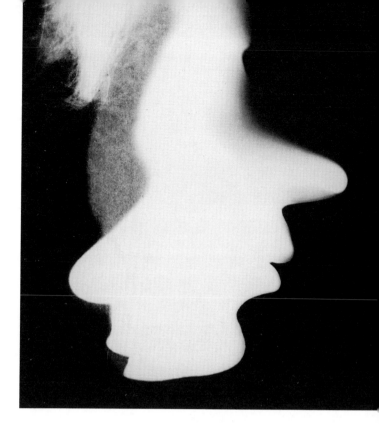

Word: Hauntology

The study of cultural ghosts

Etymology: A neologism attributed to the French philosopher Jacques Derrida, "hauntology" is an Anglicized version of the French term *hantologie,* which was a central concept in Derrida's 1993 book, *Specters of Marx: The State of the Debt, the Work of Mourning and the New International.* It combines the French verb *hanter,* to haunt, with the Greek suffix *-logie,* which refers to any logical discourse. It is crucial to recognize Derrida's play on words here: In French, *hantologie,* with its silent "h," sounds very much like *ontologie,* to which it is closely related.

Meaning: If ontology is the philosophical study of being, hauntology focuses on being as inflected by what does not exist. Logic suggests that reality encompasses all that is perceptible, measurable and present in the world; our experience, however, always contains traces of unreality. It isn't necessary to believe in ghosts and hauntings to understand this. Memory is an example of a specter that troubles the present. Memory carries forward people, events and conditions that no longer exist, embedding their absence in the present. Neither real nor unreal, these speculative sides of existence are, nevertheless, crucial to our understanding of being.

Marxist literary critic Pierre Macherey explains, "The new science of spirit Derrida undertakes to promote, by opposing to the certainties of ontology the fictions of his 'hauntology', leads to the affirmation of the reciprocal communication of the material and ideal." This affirmative aspect of Derrida's study belies a common understanding of "haunting," in which unquiet waifs disturb and undermine the present. Hauntology, by contrast, uses phantoms to help build a more comprehensive idea of being than is possible within frameworks that insist that seeing is believing.

A word as provocative as "hauntology" is ripe for appropriation. The term has been used in many fields, particularly media and music, to offer a sense that the past shimmers in the present. Hauntology in these fields is not primarily about reviving old ideas, though; instead, it aims to bring forward the fading but persistent presence of the past. The term is most closely related to a trend in British electronic music that incorporates old rhythms and melodies, sampled recordings and forgotten ambient sounds, such as the hisses and pops of vinyl, to create new compositions. Its eerie, nostalgic atmospheres conjure a sense of loss, contrasting perhaps with Derrida's more optimistic use of the term.

Words by Alex Anderson

Consider the Turtleneck

The evolution of an elite staple.

For such an unfussy garment, the history of the turtleneck is a strange one. First worn as a protective layer between chain mail and knights' delicate necks, it was then adopted by sailors and merchant marines as insulation against frigid ocean squalls. Now, it has become a signifier. Of what? That seems to change as often as the sea wind.

The turtleneck has had so many iconic moments that it's hard to conjure up just one. Steve Jobs comes to mind, of course. So do Audrey Hepburn and Michel Foucault.[1] Ask an octogenarian and they'll likely weave a tale of some dreamy beatnik with whom they locked eyes in the late 1950s.

The turtleneck's utilitarian nature lent itself to the person who wished to be seen as political, nonconforming, unconcerned with fashion, and even uninterested in sex. For the Beats and the Black Panthers, it represented a rejection of the stuffy suit-and-tie normal majority. Despite itself, though, the black beatnik turtleneck *is* sexy—figure-hugging and face-framing—as memorably demonstrated by both Marilyn Monroe and Jayne Mansfield.

Steve Jobs' uniform—a custom black mock turtleneck by Japanese designer Issey Miyake, of which he had 100 identical pieces—was intended to telegraph the same beatnik nonconformism. It was a plain garment, but Jobs' genius was that he put it on to stand out in Silicon Valley's sea of polo shirts and pocket protectors. His personal aesthetic, like that of his company, set a precedent. It was so successful that modern-day tech grifters Elizabeth Holmes, the disgraced health-tech CEO, and Markus Braun, the Austrian ex-CEO of Wirecard, currently in custody accused of fraud on an enormous scale, ripped off the style exactly. The turtleneck's cachet of nonchalant cool carried them along for a while, but eventually both had to face the music. In court, Holmes wore a gray blazer and slightly rumpled blue shirt. Her days of thinking different, it would seem, are over.[2]

Words by Stephanie d'Arc Taylor

NOTES

1. In the 1957 movie *Funny Face*, Audrey Hepburn plays Maggie Prescott, a fashion magazine editor looking for the next big trend. "The pullover with a high collared neck still has a powerful allure that communicates, 'I'm different,'" Hepburn's character says in the movie.

2. Even after the downfall of Theranos, the legacy of Elizabeth Holmes' simple black turtleneck has endured. Her trademark look has become such a popular Halloween outfit that in 2019, *Quartz* reported that "Bay Area Uniqlos are sold out of Elizabeth Holmes costumes."

Square Spaces

On internet aesthetics.

In the beginning man created the internet. The white space was without form, and blankness was upon the face of the screen. And man said, "Let there be text," and there was text. On the second day he divided the internet into pages. He connected them with blue hyperlinks, and he saw that they were good. On the third day he created GIFs—looping videos of laughing babies and dancing Jesuses that shimmied across the page. He wasn't sure if they were good, but he kept them anyway. On the following days he created embedded video, comment sections and parallax scrolling. Then man handed over the tools of creation so any human could make their own website, and a great diversity of artistic endeavor did proliferate across the web. Or rather, it proliferated until around 10 years ago, when the internet's aesthetic diversity started to wane. A recent Indiana University study surveyed 10,000 websites and found a steady increase in website layout similarity since 2010. You know the formula: A company's website opens onto a full-width image sporting overlaid text. Click the menu bar at the top or scroll down for pithy summaries of services on a tasteful bed of blank space. Everything on the internet looks the same.

This is because the way we build websites has changed. Once you needed to be fluent in JavaScript or HTML to make a site, and each page looked distinct since it was built from scratch. Now anyone can use a template on Squarespace, or, if you're a professional, popular software library Bootstrap, which is the framework used for around 20% of the roughly 1.5 billion websites in existence. Since everyone is making their sites using the same tools and templates, the creeping similarity is hardly surprising.

Websites naturally mimic each other anyway: companies want newcomers to be able to intuitively find the information they're looking for. They follow cycles in design trends, which have progressed from the glossy 3D effects of mid-2000s web 2.0 to the current fashion for flat layouts and bold block colors.

We may reminisce about the early days of the internet, when "web-surfers" built GeoCities pages in an arms race of garish colors and unforgivable fonts. Back then, the internet meant democratizing information and fostering communities that transcended national borders. MySpace encouraged users to customize their pages with music and personalized backgrounds. The corporate aesthetic of its successor, Facebook, marked a change in the ethos of the web: Companies now understood how to monetize their platforms by selling advertising space and user data. From then on, the appearance of websites became more about profitability than aesthetics, with layouts precisely calibrated to juice visitors of every last drop of their valuable attention. Our creativity is no longer presented in our own spaces, but parcelled into boxes on interchangeable social media platforms. We can project individuality into the content, but not the form.

Perhaps this is natural. Aren't websites, after all, tools for transmitting information rather than artworks? Nobody questions why books have all looked the same for the past 500 years. Still, when browsing screenshots of the early internet, it's easy to mourn those outlandish rhapsodies in media. We understand the internet is no longer beautiful because it is no longer personal. And yet, this might still change. Websites are ephemeral, constantly overwriting their own history and leaving no trace. The generic blandness of the contemporary web, too, shall pass.

On the seventh day of creation, man stopped to rest. But the internet never rests. It keeps iterating, accelerating and transforming, long after day is done.

Words by Tom Faber

HIGH FIDELITY
by John Clifford Burns

As the domination of on-demand, on-device TV services continues to grow, watching television has become an increasingly solitary activity—or else one so fraught with choice that it's hard to agree with friends or family on what to watch. There is much to be said for the lost Sunday night ritual of gathering around the television together; the anticipation of a shared cliff-hanger and, more broadly, the idea that public service broadcasting should be about giving people things they don't yet know they will like (a stark contrast to the algorithmic workings of streaming services). So, among the endless choices currently available, it's worth remembering that there always remains one more: leaving it all to chance. (Pictured: The Serif, designed by Ronan & Erwan Bouroullec for Samsung.)

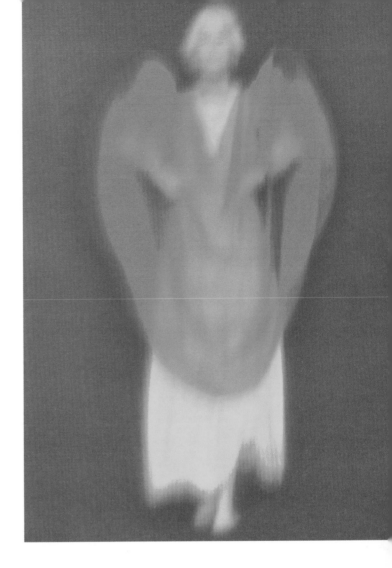

Ghosts in the Machine

How to die online.

An automatic birthday reminder for a dead friend pops up on your phone. It's a shock. Or worse: you get a Facebook message "from" that friend. They call you on Skype. They message your Gmail account. But it's only a glitch, or a hacked account. It happens with surprising frequency. Silicon Valley is still catching up with how to secure, close or help pass on social media accounts once their owners die.

It can feel outrageous to consider social media as it relates to death. The former seems so trivial, the latter so momentous. But social media accounts often contain the final vestiges of our self—our face, our interests, our friends, our voice. We work so hard to make our accounts reflect an idealized version of who we are; if we delete them, are we robbing ourselves of our most rose-tinted in memoriam?

What's the solution? Get rid of our social accounts entirely? Leave them be? Some people are betting on the prospect of a digital afterlife—enrolling in a number of new services that will post content after they're gone. (Sharing an inspirational quote from beyond the grave toes the rare line between disturbing, bizarre and—maybe—moving.)

There's no right answer of course, but as we spend more time on social media, it becomes only more important in the face of death. We live in a world populated by abandoned digital graves—defunct websites, 404 errors. We can avoid that fate by keeping our social media accounts open even after we're gone. Loved ones could write on our walls, tag us in tweets, see our photos, leave us a comment. This sort of dialogue with the departed is encouraged at analog funerals. Now, it can happen any time, any day. Forever.
Words by Cody Delistraty

Priya Ahluwalia

Meet the Londoner fashioning dazzling menswear from other designers' offcuts.

2020 marked even more of an upheaval for Priya Ahluwalia than for most. In April, the London-based menswear designer was a joint winner of the LVMH Prize alongside seven others, after it was announced that the award would be shared due to the economic strain faced by young designers during the pandemic. While finalists for the prize—which has helped launch the careers of Simon Porte Jacquemus and Grace Wales Bonner—can typically expect a barrage of press trips and photo shoots, the worldwide standstill meant back-to-back interviews over FaceTime and Zoom instead. The exhibition Ahluwalia had planned to accompany her new photography book, *Jalebi*, now sits online in a VR gallery.

It seems unlikely that any of this will stand in the way of the 27-year-old's ascent. The fashion industry is currently facing a reckoning, with its biggest names being accused of racism and elitism, and ongoing investigations into fast fashion supply chains. Ahluwalia's brand, meanwhile, represents an approach to luxury that feels fresh and inclusive. Since graduating with an MA in menswear from the University of Westminster, the designer has carved out a space for herself with her sustainable use of deadstock fabric (leftover textiles discarded by other fashion houses) and striking imagery that reflects her Indian-Nigerian heritage. As part of her prize, she's set to receive mentorship from a selection of fashion stalwarts—but it's this self-aware upstart who looks to be forging a blueprint for her old-world peers.

> ## "I'm never going to tell a single mother with two children not to buy fast fashion, because it's so much more convoluted than that. It's not the customer's responsibility—it's the company's."

FA: *Your heritage and childhood memories play a big part in your work. What sort of fashion imagery do you remember from growing up?* **PA:** I used to watch a lot of music videos on MTV Base at my house, and I loved looking at the graphics, the fashion, the cinematography. I also grew up around different cultures. On the Indian side of my family, if there was a wedding, it was a big extravaganza where you'd go to Southall to get an outfit. Likewise, on my Nigerian side, if there's an engagement party, the bride and groom will decide on a fabric for their side of the family and then you can basically order that fabric and get something made. Growing up, I was used to getting dressed up properly.

FA: *You've visited both countries many times. How have they inspired your work?* **PA:** It's inspired everything! In India, there is a massive push for supporting local artisans. You see so many beautiful textiles and techniques, and there's just a vibrancy and an energy—the hustle doesn't stop. It's the same with Lagos in Nigeria—it's such a vibrant, busy city. In both countries, I could be looking at what they're selling in the markets, what people are wearing, or it could even be down to something like the color of sand.

FA: *What was it about menswear in particular that initially excited you?* **PA:** There's just so much that's been done in womenswear, whereas men have been wearing the same clothes for about 50 years, so there's scope to push the boundaries.

FA: *Do you get a lot of women who buy it also?* **PA:** Yeah, loads of women wear it. I wear it all the time. I got tagged in a picture of IAMDDB wearing a full look from SS20, and that was amazing. A lot of people have asked me to do womenswear, so it's definitely going to be coming out of the brand soon.

FA: *You're known for your use of deadstock fabric. Do you tend to seek out specific textiles, or use what you find as a jumping-off point?* **PA:** It's a mixture of both. Some seasons, I know I want to use corduroy or camel or denim, and so I'll seek out something. Other times, I've gone and looked around at stuff and then been like, "Okay, this could be quite a moment." I like the surprises that come with not necessarily knowing the plan from start to finish.

FA: *What are the challenges of only using deadstock fabrics? Do you ever find it limiting?* **PA:** The hardest bit is falling in love with something and struggling to find more. For example, I developed my SS20 collection last summer, when there was loads of light gray tracksuit around, and then when it got to production and I was trying to source it in September, everything was black and navy. It was a nightmare! And yes, there are limitations but at the same time, you can make anything from anything. You just have to be a bit more creative in how you can make something look fresh.

FA: *You're often labeled a streetwear designer. Do you think that's accurate?* **PA:** I hate the word streetwear, to be honest. I think it's the same as the word "urban"—you basically get called a streetwear designer if you're Black. I've done a couple of tracksuits, but I also do loads of tailoring and beading and knitwear. I feel like it's one of those things that we say that's just quite lazy.

FA: *The world of fashion has faced accusations of racism, elitism and exploitative supply chains this year. How are you feeling about the industry and where your label sits amid all that?* **PA:** [The idea of luxury fashion being elitist] is something I've grappled with myself, because I want to design nice stuff that's beautifully made, and that people will keep forever. What I take issue with are the brands that sell clothes super cheaply; that to me is more "exclusionary"—not for the customers, but for the people that have to bead that fabric, dye that fabric, sew that fabric, ship that dress. It actually infuriates me. At the same time, I'm never going to tell a single mother with two children not to buy fast fashion, because it's so much more convoluted than that. It's not the customer's responsibility—it's the company's. All I can do is try and make sure my business isn't complicit.

FA: *You've just moved into your first studio. Are you happy to finally have your own space?* **PA:** For the past two years, I've been working from my family home in a spare room that I converted into a studio. I've got a great family that's supportive of me and I've been able to save on rent, and I'm really grateful for that. But at the same time I was outgrowing it. And it was impossible to find a balance: My intern and studio manager would leave, and I'd still be working until 10 p.m. I've recently moved into a new space that's really spacious, with great lighting, and it just feels like the next stage for my business. I'm happy that I now have a place to work, and then I can go home and switch off.

Interview by Fedora Abu

Ahluwalia started her brand from a spare room in her parents' home in south London. Earlier this year, she moved operations to her first studio (pictured right): "I was outgrowing it," she says.

JALEBI
by John Clifford Burns

In June 2020, Ahluwalia published *Jalebi*—her second, limited-edition photography book. Working with photographer Laurence Ellis, Ahluwalia explores what it means to be a young mixed heritage person living in modern Britain and the ways in which her own background has influenced her creative output. The publication also includes old family photographs and extracts from an interview Ahluwalia made with her grandmother about the family's experience between India and the UK.

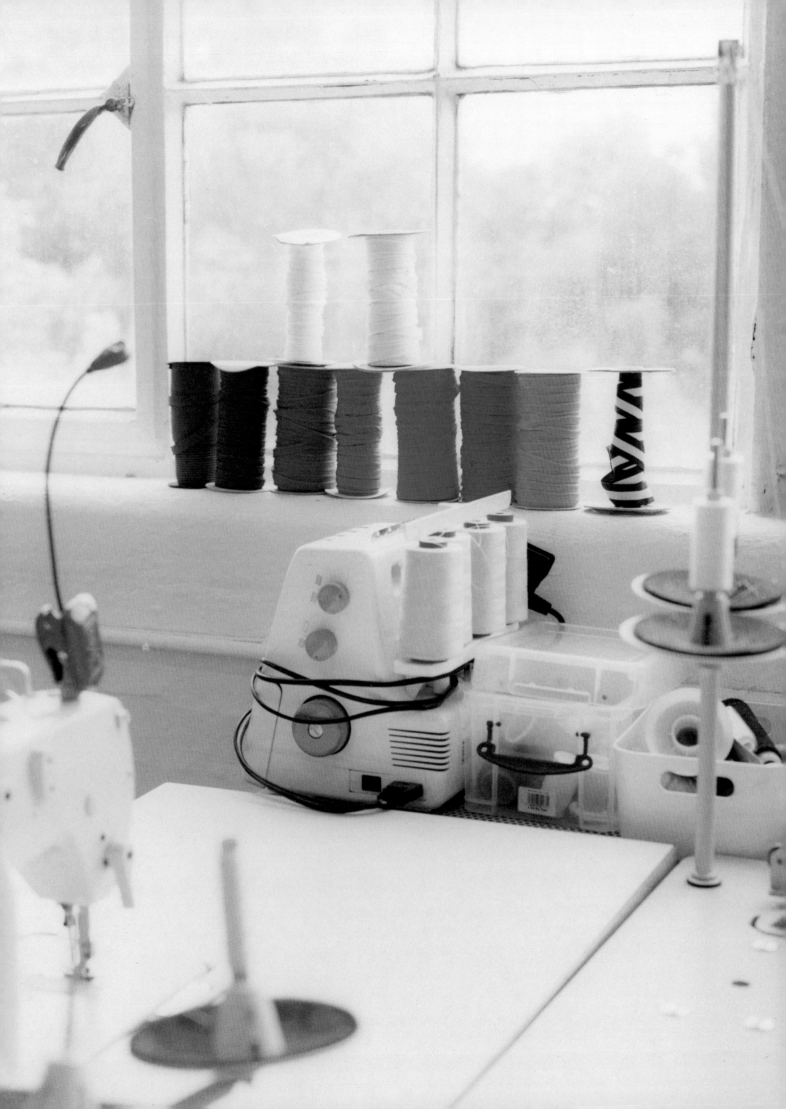

Can bad weather conjure good moods? Between the 1950s and 1980s, scientists dedicated significant resources to studying whether the cheer that many of us feel during storms is the result of a more precise mechanism than mere "cozy vibes." The theory advanced by biometeorologists (those who study the effects of weather on organisms and ecosystems) relates to the perceived effect of negative ions in the atmosphere. Negative ions are invisible molecules that have gained an extra electron. They occur naturally but are created in particular abundance by some meteorological events including downpours and lightning. Their existence is not in doubt. What is less clear is their precise effect. In one study, researchers exposed people with seasonal affective disorder to high concentrations of negative ions and found that it did indeed reduce associated symptoms. But other trials produced less persuasive and less replicable results and, critically, scientists were never able to pin down exactly how the negative ions were interacting with their subjects' mood. In 1983, the New Age writer Fred Soyka published *The Ion Effect*, in which he attributed most modern-day woes to ionic imbalance. According to a 2016 investigation published in *Nautilus* magazine, this sounded the death-knell-by-association for ions as a serious field of inquiry. Today, ionized water filtration systems and air purifiers have become the territory of dubious multi-level marketing schemes. But, expensive scams aside, it's hard to dismiss a framework that encourages us to point our noses toward stimulating weather conditions. So, forget the "calm before the storm," throw on your raincoat and seek out the calm that comes during. *Words by Harriet Fitch Little*

Divided Attention

On the everyday enigma of selective hearing.

It's a phenomenon that has long fascinated the scientific community: When in a noisy, crowded room, a person will still prick up their ears if their name is mentioned. Equally, two guests can isolate what the other says from the surrounding cacophony. They are able to engage in a private conversation without speaking louder than those around them. This is known as the "cocktail party effect," but it was air traffic controllers, not socialites, who led to its study in the 1950s after they reported finding it very difficult to listen to multiple pilots speaking at the same time through a single loudspeaker. British engineer Colin Cherry set out to understand which factors made selective hearing possible.

"It is an extraordinarily complex feat that allows the brain to 'demix' the different voices, particularly when the sound energy is overlapping and coming from a single direction," explains Dr. Edward Chang, a professor and vice chair of neurological surgery at the University of California, San Francisco, and one of the scientists whose research has shown how we process speech from two simultaneous sources.[1] According to his team's findings, the brain selectively extracts a single speaker's voice—grouping and tuning into the speech parts we choose to follow—while blocking out the other, as if it was not there. To a certain extent, this can be compared to the way our brains make it easier for us to see objects we reasonably expect to see, which means that if they are oversized, or shaped in an unexpected fashion, they become practically invisible to us.[2] "What we hear isn't the same as what sounds enter your ears," Dr. Chang says—much like what we see isn't the same as all the information our eyes can grasp.

This filter shapes our perception of the world, making it manageable for our brains to process the large amounts of information our senses are constantly bombarded with. But it means we may miss out on messages which we automatically set on "mute." For scientists and developers, the shortcuts our brains use to process information are something of a superpower. Our ability to pick what information to focus on sets us apart from machines: Despite all the advances in speech recognition technology, selective hearing remains a challenge for computers to perform. Let's appreciate our ability to quite literally sort through the noise—and prick up our ears at the merest murmur of relevant gossip.

Words by Daphnée Denis

NOTES

1. Selective attention begins at an early age: Babies will turn their heads toward a sound that is familiar to them, such as their parents' voices, indicating that even infants can selectively attend to specific stimuli among background noise.

—

—

2. In a study into how humans often miss objects that are right in front of them, Miguel Eckstein, a psychologist at the University of California, gave participants one second to find an object in a computer-rendered scene. When objects were rendered larger than life, participants missed them about 13% more than normal-sized objects.

Memes of Communication

NOTES

1. One of Blank's books, *Slender Man Is Coming*, explores the digital folklore of Slender Man—the internet bogeyman circulated in countless online posts. Slender Man is perhaps the most well-known example of Creepypasta, a horror genre derived from "copypasta," which in turn derived from the phrase "copy/paste."

2. Since 2000, the Library of Congress has employed a small team of archivists to catalog internet culture, including defunct blogs, chat rooms, webcomics and tweets. The library has already amassed more than 2.129 petabytes of data—equivalent to 18 billion digital documents.

If Oscar Wilde were still around today, he would have something perfectly scathing to say about memes. But while the viral images that clog our feeds may be considered the lowest form of culture, they aren't totally dissimilar from Wilde's own aphorisms. Both thrive on wit and concision, while revealing truths we're loathe to admit. Over the past decade, academics have been taking the world of memes more seriously via the study of digital folklore. The practice takes an anthropologist's lens to emojis, GIFs and Reddit posts, using them as clues to help understand our digitally mediated culture. Trevor Blank is a folklorist and associate professor of communication at the State University of New York at Potsdam, who has written or edited seven books about digital folklore.[1] *Interview by Tom Faber*

TF: *Some might think "digital folklore" is a contradiction in terms. What's your definition of folklore?* **TB:** I think of it as "informal traditional culture." It's the way people get around the corporate or institutionalized aspects of culture and make things their own. Folklorists are interested in how people express themselves: the songs they write, the jokes they tell, the fashions and architectures they create outside the official canon.

TF: *How does folklore travel?* **TB:** It passes through conduits. Folklore has to mean something to somebody in order to be passed along, otherwise it filters out and dies. In the past that was done through oral traditions: The conduits were the people who told and heard stories.

TF: *And today the conduits are posts on 4chan, Reddit and Twitter?* **TB:** Yes, although it's not always easy to tell where something originates online. Instead of focusing too much on where things come from, we look at what they mean and how they're being used.

TF: *What's the biggest change the internet brought about in how folklore operates?* **TB:** There's the speed at which folklore can be transmitted, the ability to connect to anyone beyond physical boundaries and the range of choice of what you can see. Instead of a small town or city, you're part of a global network of people and ideas. These are the same factors that led to a surge in conspiracy theories. There's also access to new technologies, like photo editing software. Previously there were a lot of consumers of digital folklore but few creators. Now anybody can edit pictures or use meme generator websites. Folklore is about creating meaning. Why do people post these things? Is this a subtle subconscious performance? What are they trying to reveal to themselves?

TF: *Tell me about a digital folkloric tradition.* **TB:** One example is fake Amazon product reviews. In 2011, students were protesting at UC Davis and a cop pepper sprayed them. He became a meme—the "casually pepper spray everything cop." People found the exact model of pepper spray he used and left satirical reviews on Amazon saying that it was great for squashing free speech or getting hippies off your lawn. A moment of national debate was playing out and it's still there now, archived under the pepper spray. These kinds of mock reviews have been used for over 15 years as a form of folk protest.

TF: *Where are the main repositories of digital folklore?* **TB:** There are user-curated sites like Urban Dictionary and Know Your Meme, which aren't run by folklorists. The Library of Congress is also creating an internet archive of websites and online materials.[2]

TF: *Do you think people should be going out of their way to preserve artifacts of digital folklore or is it natural that some are remembered and others just fade away?* **TB:** I tend to say capture as much as you can. Even the stuff that doesn't make it to the top tier still tells us about a particular moment and time. In a way with social media, we all become digital archivists and curators. With our social media presences, we all create a museum of ourselves.

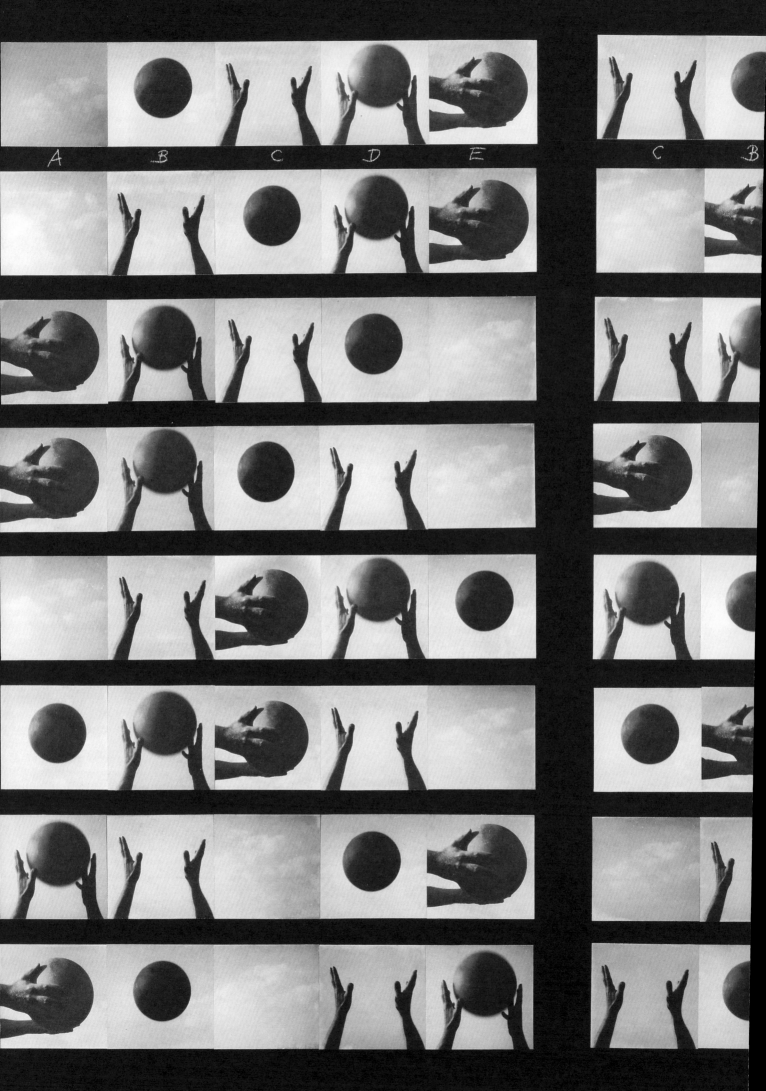

Photograph: Dóra Maurer, Reversible and Interchangeable Phases of Motion No. 6, 1972. Courtesy of József Rosta / Ludwig Museum

On Principle

The utility of thought experiments.

The philosopher Stefano Gualeni isn't your grandmother's intellectual. Sure, he produces papers, gives lectures and mentors students. But he also builds things. His creations, which he believes can fulfill the ultimate goal of the humanities, are a far cry from the traditional output of philosophers. Gualeni's ultimate tool to trigger people to become better thinkers is a video game about soup.

The game, called *Something Something Soup Something*, asks players to imagine that it is the year 2078, and their job is to oversee the output of alien workers on a planet colonized by Earth. Being aliens, though, they don't always understand the task at hand. The player's job is to categorize individual items the aliens produce—from "a foamy liquid with batteries and croutons served in a hat with a fork" to "a thick liquid with mushrooms served in a coconut with a spoon"—as soup or not soup. At the end of the game, a player's individual criteria for soup are presented. These can include "A soup can be served in anything" or "A soup must be completely edible."

Gualeni's game, and others like it, are versions of the classic philosopher's thought experiment, updated for the digital age. Their goal is to help thinkers puzzle out their views on thorny theoretical questions. "These hypothetical situations," says Gualeni, "challenge us to perform mental exercises about those situations and think through their various consequences."

Thought experiments have often been used as teaching aids. The Schrödinger's cat puzzle, for instance, is designed to make quantum mechanics digestible for laypeople by envisioning the mortality of a hapless feline.[1] Other thought experiments are meant to provoke questions of morality. The trolley problem asks you to make a decision about a trolley careering out of control toward a group of five people tied to the tracks. Do you do nothing, and allow the trolley to hit the five people? Or do you pull a lever to divert the trolley, sealing the fate of only one unlucky soul nearby instead of the other five?

Quantum mechanics may be the purview of a lofty few, but ethics are more relevant than ever—all the more so, Gualeni says, as the march of technology takes us into increasingly muddy terrain. Indeed, the MIT Moral Machine asks players to make similar life-or-death decisions as the trolley problem, for the purposes of gathering data for autonomous car algorithms. In the game, your choice to run over a grandmother or a toddler may eventually inform "decisions" made by future self-driving cars.[2]

Just as Plato's cave allegory isn't really about a cave, *Something Something Soup Something* isn't really about soup. "The political and social crisis we're now facing is perhaps a product of us not focusing on social accountability and the formation of citizens," Gualeni says. By exploding people's idea of soup, he believes, he can challenge them to think more critically about their other beliefs. "It's making people conscious of ideas they had never reflected upon. It's a valuable goal in itself."
Words by Stephanie d'Arc Taylor.

NOTES

1. Schrödinger's cat imagines a theoretical cat and a radioactive source, released at random, in a sealed box. As it is impossible to know if the cat is dead or alive unless the box is opened, then the cat is (in a sense) both dead and alive. The principle demonstrates the eccentricity of a certain school of quantum physics: that scientific theories are neither right nor wrong until tested and proved.

2. A 2016 study by the researchers at MIT Moral Machine found that the majority of participants approved of autonomous vehicles that would sacrifice passengers for the greater good and would like others to buy them. But the study also indicated that they would refuse to purchase such a car themselves, preferring to buy a car that protected them first. In other words, people refused to buy the car they found to be more ethical.

THE PROPOSAL

by John Clifford Burns

When the architect Luis Barragán died in 1988, his last testament cleaved his archive into two: His personal effects were to remain at Casa Luis Barragán, his personal residence (pictured; now a museum and UNESCO World Heritage Site); his professional archive, including the rights to his name and work (and all photographs taken of it) were sold. They ended up in the hands of Fererica Zanco, who, it is rumored, acquired them as an engagement gift from her fiancé, the chairman of a Swiss furniture company, in the mid-1990s. Zanco then kept the archives publicly inaccessible for the next 20 years. Enter Jill Magid—a writer and artist who once trained as a spy. Faced with major obstacles when mounting her own exhibition on Barragán, she began making *The Proposal* (2019)— a feature-length documentary about her attempt to emancipate the archive from what she viewed as Zanco's rigid corporate control. The documentary follows a three-year correspondence between the two women and questions how power, public access and copyright construct an artist's legacy, before building to a ghoulish denouement: Magid presents Zanco with the gift of a two-carat diamond made from the cremated remains of Barragán's body that she had set into a ring, in exchange for the return of his archive to Mexico—a poetic counterproposal to the offer of marriage that landed Zanco with the files. *Photograph by Salva Lopez (© Luis Barragan/VISDA)*

Eric Nam

A reeducation in K-pop from one its brightest stars.

Before debuting his first single in 2013, Atlanta-born Eric Nam worked in New York City at a local consulting firm. Scared by the prospect of settling down, he decided to give singing a go. "I kept thinking, Can I be experimental and pursue my passions and dreams? So I took a year off," he says. When he made it to the top five in one of South Korea's leading talent shows, he moved to Seoul where he was hailed as one of K-pop's most promising solo acts. On the phone from his apartment, he explains how a lack of Asian stars in the US brought him to South Korea, and what it means to be a solo K-pop artist in an industry dominated by sharply choreographed groups. *Interview by Gabriele Dellisanti*

GD: *Did you grow up knowing you wanted to become a singer?* **EN:** I think it's one of those things you always know you want to be, but to me, probably like to many others, it always felt like a naive aspiration. I never really thought that it could happen.

    GD: *Why were you doubtful that you could make it?* **EN:** I grew up never seeing an Asian face on TV or film, so why would it be acceptable for me to do music? I think people only dream of what they can really envision. For music in particular, the only place I saw any Asians was in Korea or when I would rent VHS tapes to watch Korean TV shows.

    GD: *Do you think the situation has improved since?* **EN:** Even to this day, there are very few Asian acts in the US. I hope that when the next 13-year-old Asian Justin Bieber looks at the world and asks if they can do this, they can see people like me or bands like BTS and think, Yes, let's give it a shot.[1]

    GD: *Do you define your music as K-pop?* **EN:** If you look at the definition of K-pop, it is popular music that is made in Korea. But the Western perception of it is 13 guys with purple hair wearing pink jackets, all dancing and looking the same. And it's funny because I think my music is nothing but American pop sung in Korean. Here people listen to my music and would never call it K-pop—they just say it sounds incredibly American! [When I first moved here] I could barely speak Korean, meaning that I spent a good half of my time feeling like an idiot because I didn't know what was going on.

    GD: *What's your experience of the industry been like?* **EN:** Unfortunately, in the West there is a negative perception of the industry as a machine. It is not perfect, but in my experience in Korea the craft is taken incredibly seriously; [there's] a work ethic that is part of the culture. And it is this work ethic that has oftentimes been characterized as very negative.[2] [But] I know for sure that for my friends in the US music industry, the reality isn't any better.

NOTES

1. The global image of K-Pop is maturing. BTS, arguably the biggest boy band in the world, announced a surprise collaboration earlier this year with renowned British artist Antony Gormley. As part of Connect BTS, a global art initiative, the band commissioned Gormley's work *New York Clearing*—an immersive installation of tangled aluminum tubing on New York City's Pier 3.

2. A recent spate of suicides among South Korean musicians has brought the spartan regimens and dark underbelly of the K-pop industry to light. "Theirs is a profession especially vulnerable to psychological distress," Lee Hark-joon, co-author of *K-Pop Idols: Popular Culture and the Emergence of the Korean Music Industry*, told *The New York Times* in 2019.

Fish Out of Water

On unexpected animal encounters.

Children walking in the forest don't censor their expectations when it comes to animals. They hope to see not just foxes and owls, but lions, polar bears, and goblins too. As we grow older, our encounters with animals become more rote—we know what's around, and what isn't.

Which is why it's such a delight to occasionally see animals out of place. Looking up from a drink in Telegraph Hill, for example, to hear San Francisco's parrots squawking through the fog. Or coming upon wild pigs crowding a beach in the Bahamas. These oddities revive old hopes that anything can happen.

London, a city that has hosted exiles for centuries, is home to thousands of rose-ringed parakeets. How these nonmigratory African birds arrived in Britain is a matter of debate. Some say the original mating pair were released on Carnaby Street by a prankish Jimi Hendrix. Others say a flock escaped from the set of *The African Queen* in 1951. Though the parakeets are loved by some, many consider them an invasive nuisance, and have sought for years to cull them. Britain's parakeets are largely benign. But other nonnative species do represent a genuine threat to biodiversity. The venomous brown tree snake, for instance, decimated the bird population of Guam after arriving there in the 1950s.

Local reactions to these phenomena are often colored by unconscious prejudice. Whether we realize it or not, our fears about parakeets and tree snakes sometimes hum the melodies of xenophobia. It is healthy, then, to learn the scientific distinction between invasive and nonnative species. Tomatoes, native only to South America, did not arrive in Italy until the 16th century, and were not cooked until much later—due in part to a popular myth that the strange fruits were poisonous. Basil, which originated either in India or China, travelled to Europe earlier, along eastern trade routes. Caprese, therefore, is at once a quintessentially Italian and comprehensively nonnative dish.

To qualify as "invasive," a nonnative species has to displace or destroy one or more native species. And that makes it a very poor metaphor for human migration. A simple habit worth cultivating: Question anyone who says newcomers will erase what you love, and always remember that you—a confluence of identities and pollinations beyond count—are also a parakeet of sorts.
Words by Asher Ross

TAKE A SEAT
by John Clifford Burns

We often use human terms to describe the ways that chairs are designed; they have "arms" and "legs" and "backs." It is not such a leap, then, to consider why we associate certain chairs with certain people—and our memories of them. An example: Marty Crane's putrid-green armchair, which took center-stage on the set of *Frasier*. In one episode, when Frasier replaces the chair, Marty reveals how chairs become imbued with memory: "I'll tell you what chair I want... I want the chair I was sitting in the night you called me to tell me I had a grandson. I want the chair I was in all those nights, when your mother used to wake me up with a kiss," he says. Over time, chairs become imprinted with the shape of our lives. They are one of the most personal pieces of furniture we can choose. (Pictured: Luna Chair in moss velvet by Mitchell Gold + Bob Williams.)

Gold Diggers

Buried treasure originates and ends in misfortune. The standard tale starts with calamity: Privateers ransack a merchant ship, then wreck themselves on jagged shoals. A survivor buries the plunder before returning to civilization, but hard living prevents its recovery. Deathbed revelations to a trusted friend offer cryptic instructions—a hint hoarsely whispered, a crudely scrawled cipher, a map sketched on parchment. The eager recipient exhausts finances and sanity seeking untold wealth, then passes the dream on. At last, a dogged scavenger hunts down and digs up the treasure.

The thrill of the quest is undeniable. Struggle and tragedy fade in the light of gold, of wealth beyond imagining… Well, enough to cover the costs, and maybe the legal fees. The ancient principle of "finders keepers" may apply when swinging a metal detector over the beach, but it breaks down when values go up. UNESCO conventions protect cultural heritage; property owners get a cut; appraisers charge a fee; governments tax the gains. When Bobby Pritchett discovered a 16th-century French ship sunken near Florida, he found himself in conflict with UNESCO, the US and France, and ultimately lost not only the bounty but the millions that investors had poured into his search.

The quest for treasure often exacts more than financial costs. When art dealer Forrest Fenn cached a treasure chest in the Rocky Mountains and published clues to its location in his memoir, aptly named *The Thrill of the Chase*, he launched a decade-long frenzy. Thousands of people searched for it, many ruining marriages and exhausting retirement funds. Five hunters died trying before someone found the chest in 2020, suggesting that, while the allure of treasure may be great, prudence recommends leaving it buried.

Words by Alex Anderson

Wigmaker, hairstylist and head prop maker Tomihiro Kono is a master of disguise. His ethereal headwear has long been key to the visual identity of Comme des Garçons' runway and has appeared on the covers of *W*, *T Magazine* and several global editions of *Vogue*. For all the razzle-dazzle of his astral creations, the artist himself is a reserved perfectionist. He spoke to Selena Takigawa Hoy about how a childhood on an orange farm made way for a career behind the scenes of the most glamorous shoots and shows in London, New York and Tokyo. *Interview by Selena Takigawa Hoy*

SH: *How did you become interested in hair and wigs?* **TK:** I was born and raised in Ehime, Shikoku. My parents were *mikan* [orange] farmers. I am the oldest son, and by tradition, I was supposed to take over my parents' job. But there was nothing as far as the eye could see in the countryside that looked interesting to me. The most appealing job was the hairdresser. In the country, it seemed like a shining example, a window to the art world. I thought I could escape reality and get into hair styling.

SH: *Did you ever consider any alternative careers?* **TK:** Being from the country, I love animals. I thought about being a dog groomer. I discussed that with my parents, but they said, "Dogs never say thank you." They said, "If you could do dog hair, you could do human hair." I love sea animals, insects and nature. Especially right now, deep-sea creatures, which I find fascinating.

SH: *You have quite a few punk styles in your repertoire. How did that emerge?* **TK:** I was born in the 1980s. I was influenced by punk styles because in Japan, the pop stars left an impression on me as a child— musicians like Madonna, or Cindy Lauper. Japanese pop stars and musicians were inspired by European and American artists. I started copying them at first, making those hairstyles. The Checkers, Akina Nakamori and Kyoko Koizumi were my idols. I like the shape of punk. It's very me.

SH: *You explore different personas through wigs. How can a wig change the way someone interacts with the world?* **TK:** A wig is designed to make a definite impression upon others, but also to conceal the true nature of an individual. Choosing a wig can be an act of self-assertion, self-defense and self-realization. We are highly sensitive that our character can easily be changed in response to our hairstyle, either consciously or unconsciously.

SH: *You were in New York during the height of the pandemic and initial lockdown. Tell us about your pandemic projects.* **TK:** I started posting my wigs on Instagram. I saw that some people had made filters with wigs or hairstyles. But it was too fake for me. It was two-dimensional. I saw that there was definitely space for me to do a wig filter myself. Me and my partner Sayaka Maruyama, we decided to create 10 strong characters from my wigs. And since so many people were staying home because of the pandemic, just looking at their iPhones, we got so many hits right away. I also did a mask collaboration with Collina Strada, an up-and-coming New York designer. Those were a donation, raising money for various Black Lives Matter charities.

SH: *You've lived in a few countries. How has that influenced your style?* **TK:** I get influenced by the changes in my environment. In Japan, I learned about Japanese geisha hair and trendy haircuts in Harajuku. When I was in the UK, I was more into romanticism, surrealism, and a dark, poetic, gothic aesthetic. Since I moved to New York, my style has become colorful, young and universal.

SH: *Any other favorite inspirations?* **TK:** A massive Victorian wig. I always get inspired by huge Victorian hairstyles, as they only have drawings or paintings as a record.

PERSONAS 111
by Harriet Fitch Little

In March 2020, Tomihiro Kono (pictured above) published his second photobook, *Personas 111: The Art of Wig Making 2017-2020*, in which he collected together some of his most otherworldly designs of recent years. Three days after the book came out, New York went into the first stages of lockdown against COVID-19. Regardless of the restrictions, the wigmaker had already decided to eschew the gallery installations he had planned because of the atmosphere locally. "At that time, anti-Asian hate crimes were happening in New York," he explains.

Seeing the Light

The aftermath of almost dying.

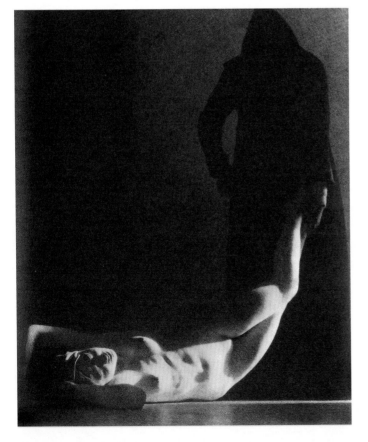

It sounds like the ending of a made-for-TV movie: On the operating table after a catastrophic medical event, a patient is suddenly thrust from their physical form and observes the scene from above, before being drawn to a dazzling white light. They pass by memories and loved ones as they move toward it, all the while overwhelmed by total joy and peace. But this isn't fiction, and it isn't an ending—the patient recovers against the odds and returns to ordinary, waking life where they recount what they perceive as a brush with heaven itself.

Thousands of people have reported near-death experiences (NDEs) since the 1970s when they were first studied seriously as a scientific and spiritual phenomenon. Experiencers, as they call themselves, reason that the consistency of their various accounts proves that they have encountered material reality. How could it be true, they argue, that people across the world see and feel the same things with such uniformity, if a simple spasm of an oxygen-deprived brain were responsible?

The truth is more complex and more interesting than the party line. NDEs are not, in fact, as uniform as organizations like the Near Death Experience Research Foundation would have you believe. Unpleasant, disturbing and even profoundly traumatic NDEs make up 23% of those referenced in the National Library of Medicine. Some experience visceral trips through what they see as hell, surrounded by tormented people in perpetual agony. Certainly this kind of NDE is less appealing to the general public who are eager to hear verifiable proof not only that the afterlife exists but that it is full of love and comfort.

Still, there is one notable commonality among those who report an NDE. Regardless of the path it took them on, they report that the experience led them to change their approach to life. Many turn to religion, while others recalibrate their priorities and focus on acts of selflessness. Those who experienced a kind of heaven had received wonderful confirmation that they were on the right path and should proceed in a virtuous manner, while those who glimpsed hell had been given a warning to turn around.

Whether or not one believes that it is possible to experience the material reality of an afterlife, the NDEs do "really" happen to experiencers. They viscerally confront the end of their life on earth. That life ends is something we all ostensibly know, but also try to effectively *not know* on a day-to-day basis. Experiencers no longer have that option and live with a genuine constant ambient awareness of death—and that's as real as it gets.

Words by Megan Nolan

Photograph: Death of Hypatia by William Mortensen, circa 1927. From American Grotesque: The Life and Art of William Mortensen. Courtesy of Feral House.

2.

Features

46 — 112

For over 25 years, America's alternative sweetheart has operated according to

M.

a simple philosophy: To live with joy, pour life's darkness into your art.

Words by Robert Ito, Photography by Emman Montalvan & Styling by Rebecca Ramsey

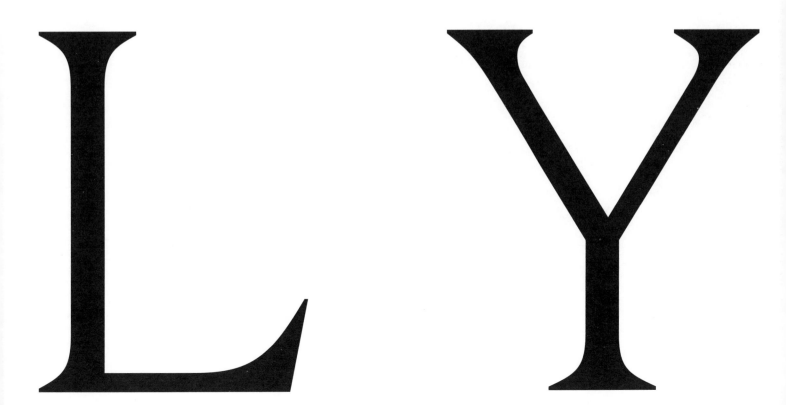

In Los Angeles, *Miranda July* talks to *Robert Ito* about pouring the fear, pleasure and unspoken weirdness of life into her genre-bending art.

Is there anything Miranda July can't do? That's not something one asks somebody without sounding like a total suck-up, so I put the question to July in a roundabout sort of way, like so: *Is there anything you tried to do, but couldn't, or did very poorly?* July considers, and allows that there was that one time in her 20s when she was going to make a trilogy of short films, but didn't. The name of the trilogy was *Modern Water*, and who knows what might have been? "I remember realizing that you can have these huge ideas and get really excited, and then absolutely fail to follow through," she says. "I remember thinking: Never do that again."

One gets the sense that she hasn't. Over the course of her three-decades-and-change artistic career, July has written books (*No One Belongs Here More Than You*, an award-winning collection of short stories; *The First Bad Man*), created multimedia theater pieces (*Love Diamond*; *The Swan Tool*), and directed films (2005's *Me and You and Everyone We Know*, which won the Caméra d'Or prize at Cannes; and 2020's *Kajillionaire*, for which the big ticket release was postponed because of COVID precautions). She has designed shoes and opened an interfaith thrift shop,

fronted indie bands and co-created a short-lived zine. At 16, she penned a play about a correspondence she had struck up with a prisoner serving a life sentence for murder; a quarter century later, she debuted an art piece based on the life of an Uber driver from West Africa whom she met while on her way to interview the pop singer Rihanna. Her works have featured sent emails, romance paperbacks and large fiberglass pieces one could stick head, arms and legs into. "Sometimes I think that, because I work in so many mediums, people aren't sure if I'm *really* a writer, or if I'm *really* a filmmaker," she says. "People really like things that are clear, and that are one thing."

July is talking about some of her past projects at Dust Studios LA, a nondescript photo studio sandwiched between an auto insurance agency and a Sit 'n Sleep mattress store. She's here for a photo shoot, so moments before, she had been sporting a Kelly green plaid jacket, purple bikini top, black bikini bottoms and heels; now, she's in a dark blue yukata-style robe dotted with tiny white flowers. Her lips are a bright red. One thing July has learned since her earliest days as an artist slash writer slash other assorted vocations, she says, is

Set Design: Gabriela Cohar Hair: Dennis Gots Makeup: Natasha Severino Nails: Naoko Saita

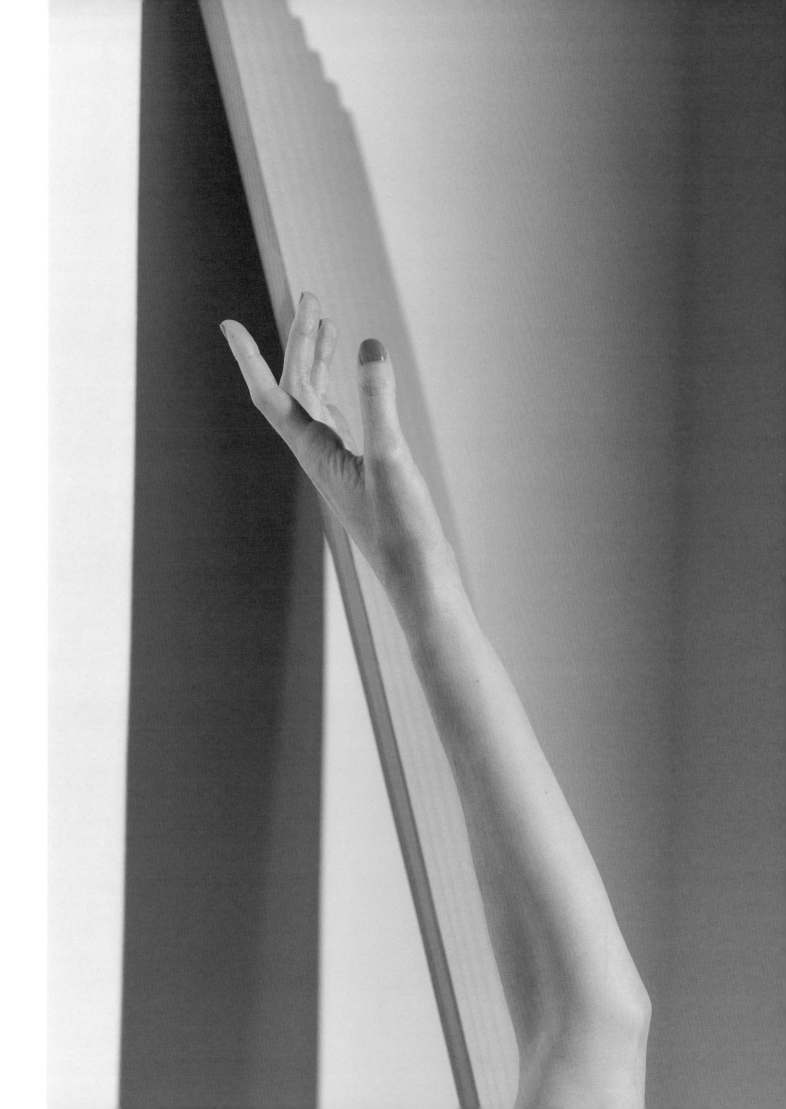

FEATURES

"the role of pleasure. Not that I wasn't having a good time, but I didn't prioritize it, and I wasn't raised to value it. I distinctly remember being sad, and my dad saying to me, 'but isn't sadness interesting?' And I agree. Sadness is interesting. So is joy. So are all the feelings."

There has never been a better time to catch up on all things Miranda July. In April 2020, Prestel published July's self-titled monograph, which features samplings of the artist's work and life (notebook entries, zine pages, film stills) alongside commentary from several of her colleagues and pals, from Rick Moody and Carrie Brownstein to Lena Dunham and Spike Jonze. *Me and You and Everyone We Know*, which launched July's feature filmmaking career and cemented her status as an indie film darling, was given the Criterion Collection treatment that same month.

When we speak in late summer, *Kajillionaire*, her third feature, is due to open in theaters in September, although COVID may delay its release. In the film, Richard Jenkins and Debra Winger play small-time grifters and cheats living in Los Angeles (their marks include an old, dying man and a small post office) who have indoctrinated their daughter, played by Evan Rachel Wood, into the family business, seemingly from birth. The parents, such as they are, seem irredeemable to me, but July, the mother of an eight-year-old child herself, is more forgiving. What mom is perfect, after all? "I can see how you might have had a weird period of time in your life where things weren't really clicking for you, or you were going through something," she says. "And that might just happen to be your kid's *whole childhood*. It would seem sort of unfair to have yourself characterized by that, by just that one weird thing you were going through."

July should be in a whirl of publicity for all three of these proj-

ects, but like much of Los Angeles, where she lives, and the rest of the world, she is currently sheltering in place, her life upended by the COVID-19 pandemic. July and her husband, the indie film director Mike Mills, are sharing parenting duties while schools and camps in town are closed, which means her work days have effectively been cut in half. "I remember days when I could get off course and have a little emotional meltdown and still have time to correct for it," she says. "That's the difference now. You either have your emotional breakdown, or you write. You're not going to do both."

Even so, she has still found time to work on another novel, and to embark on new projects through Instagram, including the first installment of Jopie—a movie performed by her followers and their families in response to her directions. She's also toiling away on projects that she can't talk about just now, and educating herself about the Black Lives Matter movement and the recent (and not-so-recent) incidents of police violence, and urging her 280,000-plus followers on Twitter and Insta-

gram to do the same. "Like many people, I'm trying to use this moment to make change where I can," July says. "This is a huge moment for civil rights. I don't want to have just been someone who clocked in and did the same thing through the revolution, you know? I'd rather be thrown about and have everything upended, even if that means some days are totally uncomfortable, and I've lost my bearings."

When *Me and You and Everyone We Know* opened in 2005, July went from Miranda July, relatively private citizen, to Miranda July, a person people felt comfortable accosting. The film, which stars July as an amateur video artist and sometime "Eldercab" driver who falls in love with a shoe salesman (John Hawkes), had an outsized impact on its critics, who praised its "sharp writing" (*The Washinton Post*) and "wide-eyed, quizzical approach to the world" (*The New York Times*). Fans tattooed the film's strangest and most enduring image—an emoticon,))<>((, meant to symbolize two people pooping into each other's butt holes, "back and forth,

Left: July wears a dickey collar by Marc Jacobs, tights by Prada and shoes by Balenciaga. Right: She wears a blouse by Gucci.

"Sadness is interesting. So is joy. So are all the feelings."

"*Part of my process is to not be self-conscious, not think about how I've made things.*"

forever"—on their wrists and feet.
July met Mills at a party at Sundance, where the film had its triumphant world premiere. "All of that began probably the same day I met him, so I could never get across to him that *literally last week* my life wasn't like this," she says. "He would never know me that way. And I was like, 'This isn't the real me! This isn't how my life has been.'"

When I ask July what it was like to go back and revisit the film that marked such a dividing line in her life, she admits she never has. "I don't really go back and watch the movies again, ever, after they premiere," she says, laughing. "I think for this [the Criterion release], I looked at some pieces on YouTube, maybe?" In retrospect, she says, "I guess I'm kind of amazed now that I got away with it."

Among the things she got away with: scenes in which a six-year-old boy engages in online sex talk with a middle-aged woman, and others in which a pair of teenage girls carry on a sexually tinged flirtation with their adult neighbor. "Occasionally I'll see someone accusing me of pedophilia or something, and I'll be like, 'Right, right,'" she says. "Because if you're only hearing about the idea of children and sexuality next to each other in terms of like, something has gone terribly wrong, then of course you would become uncomfortable, and some people were. But the other thing is, I was so young. I had been a child longer than I had been an adult. I was really writing about what I knew best at that point: being a girl, being a little kid. I knew about my own character's job, but the other jobs were more like loose sketches of what I thought adults might do."

For years after the film's release, thanks at least in part to the power of the character she played in it, July became indelibly linked in the minds of fans with the film's Christine: talented and creative, loopy and unmoored, emotionally frag-

ile. Twee. That happens less now. "I guess it's sort of a good thing, or I can feel like I've done my job well, because it used to be that people would come up to me and ask, 'Can I give you a hug?'" she says. "I guess there was something about that character that made them feel like doing that, which is so not me. I mean, anyone who knows me is like, Nope! She definitely doesn't want to give you a hug."

Desire for hugs or no, much of July's work involves the search for human connection—how much we need it and how little we ever get of it—so the confusion is perhaps understandable. It's something that infuses much of the work on display within her chronological monograph. July compares looking through the notes and journal entries and assorted artifacts of projects past to cleaning out a closet, although not in the sort of joy-sparking way that someone like professional tidier Marie Kondo might recommend. The task, she says, was excruciating. "I think it's part of my process to not be self-conscious, not think about how I've made things, or what the journey has been. I think probably for a lot of artists or writers, you'd sort of do anything not to have to needle yourself in that way."

July's eyes are closed. She's in front of the photographer, all in red now, doing cool things with her hands. Prince is playing ("1999"), then Dua Lipa ("Don't Start Now"). During breaks, she comes out to the monitor to take a peek and see how things are coming along. She's been on both sides of the camera often enough that one gets the sense she could do any number of jobs on this particular set, if called to.

But she has learned to let others take their turns and have their say. Indeed, early on in planning the new monograph, the idea was for July to write about herself, seeing as how she has been a writer for years and knows the projects

in the book better than anyone. In the end, however, she decided to let others do most of the talking; each project covered in the monograph is accompanied by the recollections of friends and collaborators. The stories they tell about July are compelling. Like that time she got caught stealing Neosporin from a grocery store and was so scared she peed on the floor (as told by Lindsay Beamish, now an assistant professor in performing arts at Emerson College), or the accounts of what she did to get by as a young artist in Portland. "There were some more revealing things that I kind of gulped and was like, Well, maybe it's okay if the world knows that," she says.

In the meantime, July is excited for people to see *Kajillionaire*, which she insists is not about her own parents, although she sees the similarities: how every family thinks their way of doing things is the right and only way, and general anxieties about money growing up. "I wrote a whole draft of that movie before it ever occurred to me that it had any relationship to me or my family," she says. She also concedes that some of the film's themes about parents and parenting come from her own fears about being a mom, and possibly messing that up herself. In many ways, she says, her films are practice runs, albeit often extreme ones, for everyday life.

"That's partly what art is for sometimes," she says. "People are still mad at me for the cat dying at the end of my movie." The film she's referring to is *The Future*, a 2011 feature in which July plays Paw Paw, an injured, talking cat, sort of, as well as the 30-something woman who hopes to adopt him. In the end, Paw Paw dies, but July just told you that herself. "And I always think, Yeah, that was horrible, but my *child* is still alive, you know?" she says. "I think I'm the kind of person who'd rather fully embody the darkness in my art so I don't do it in my life."

Home Tour: Arcosanti

Sci-fi lair, Mediterranean village, utopian ecosystem: *Tim Hornyak* peers inside Arizona's experimental desert community. Photography by *Justin Chung*

"In the desert you become a discoverer," the Lebanese American author Ameen Rihani wrote. He was alluding to the desert's power to spark spiritual awakening, but it can also produce other transformations. Situated in the Sonoran desert in Arizona, Arcosanti was founded to reconceptualize how people can live together. 2020 marks the 50th year of this bold attempt to create a new community.

Arcosanti is a collection of whimsical structures atop an isolated mesa about 60 miles north of Phoenix. There are modular block units, Romanesque half-domes and oculus windows looking out over the valley below. Circular and semicircular motifs recur in the expanse of weathered concrete. Viewed from certain angles, it could double as the lair of a Bond villain—in fact, it served as the location for the 1988 sci-fi film *Nightfall*—but overall it resembles more a Mediterranean hilltop village with a modern twist. That was part of the legacy of Italian architect Paolo Soleri, who founded Arcosanti in 1970. He conceived it as an "arcology," a concept yoking architecture and ecology, with the goal of building a compact settlement based on ecologically sound principles.

Born in Turin in 1919, Soleri moved to the US in 1947 and apprenticed with Frank Lloyd Wright at Taliesin West in Scottsdale for 18 months. Most of his work was done in the American Southwest, and Arcosanti is his magnum opus. During his lifetime, he received numerous awards and fellowships from organizations ranging from the Guggenheim Foundation to the Venice Biennale of Architecture. The *New York Times*' architecture critic Ada Louise Huxtable hailed his philosophical and environmental awareness and described Soleri as "the prophet in the desert."

When he died in 2013, he was widely eulogized. Four years later, however, his daughter Daniela Soleri publicly accused her father of sexual molestation and attempted rape when she was a teenager. "Every human endeavor is marked by at least some people whose contributions are significant and enduring but whose behaviors were, or are, anywhere from unpleasant to horrific," she wrote. The Cosanti Foundation, which oversees Arcosanti, has encouraged people to reconsider Soleri's legacy while acknowledging that "to support great ideas is not to condone the conduct of their creator."

Vast, circular windows ensure that desert light illuminates Arcosanti's interiors, lessening the project's electricity consumption.

The Ceramics Apse's half dome shape (pictured right) and its south facing position provide sufficient shelter that workshops can take place outside almost all year round.

The surrounding Sonoran Desert is a vast and diverse ecosystem home to rattlesnakes, coyotes and roadrunners. It extends southward into Mexico and covers over 100,000 square miles.

It's impossible to entirely separate the mesa from the man, because Soleri's ideals were what shaped Acrosanti. His 1970 book, *Arcology: City in the Image of Man*, denounced the urban blight of the day and dreamed of arcologies that included fantastic communities in the ocean and outer space. "Arcologies are architectural organisms of such character and dimensions as to be ecologically relevant," he wrote. "They are that architecture which is the ecology of reflective life."

With its surroundings of craggy mesas and tall Mediterranean cypresses, and its Escheresque origami of domes and cubes, Arcosanti is designed for reflection and introspection. It's both part of the ecology, especially given the fact that its concrete structures were cast using earthen molds, and very much a human landscape. "From the perspective of an architect, the site is not only formally beautiful, but empirically opportunistic," says Kevin Pappa, a onetime Arcosanti planner who worked on interior renovations during his tenure. "There is a large disconnect between architects in the field and architects in the office, and my work at Arcosanti has given me the experience to bridge the gap."

Arcosanti bills itself somewhat ironically as an urban laboratory. An antithesis to the modern city and its sprawl, it's designed to be as compact as possible—some residents have commutes of only 30 seconds to their offices—with a small environmental footprint thanks to the use of passive solar energy for part of its lighting and heating. For example, the south-facing Ceramics Apse, an open-air workshop, features shade in the summer and solar warming in the winter, when the sun is at a low angle in the sky. Some residential units are connected to greenhouses that supply them with heat as well as food. The complex grows vertically instead of horizontally and eschews roads in favor of walkways, courtyards and other public spaces: The midpoint feature of the site is the Vaults, a large arched vault that serves as a meeting area and performance space. Another open space is the Foundry Apse, where liquid bronze is poured into sand molds to create wind bells, a major source of income for the project.

The most recent structure in Arcosanti was dedicated in 1989, and the settlement is nowhere near the scale initially envisioned. Instead of 1,500 inhabitants, it is home to about 80. A few have been there for decades, while others are there temporarily for internships and workshops on subjects like metalworking and silt-casting; some 25,000 people from around the world visit annually. Architect Jeff Stein was an early convert in the 1970s, lured by Soleri's utopian vision and the commune-like atmosphere when volunteers came together to build the initial structures.

"Arcosanti represents a kind of triumph of the imagination," says Stein, a member of the Cosanti Foundation board of directors. "Cities, perhaps the newest form of life on Earth, and certainly the biggest and most expensive cultural artifact humans create, need to perform as efficiently and delightfully as the rest of life does. So, what if we could design cities in a way that conforms to how the rest of life is designed: an enormous quantity of events inside smaller and smaller quantities of material and time? Arcosanti represents a first try at this, attempting to build an understanding of 'complexity' and 'compactness' in urban design to sustain communities so we humans might thrive in them."

Ali Gibbs arrived as an education, agriculture and design student on a workshop, later staying on and working as cook, bartender, guest services steward and foundry staffer. The high desert landscape proved enthralling: "The experience of my first monsoon here, a true force of nature dumping inches of rain on the parched earth in a span of 15 minutes, giving way to a sense of relief backed by towering clouds painted in pastels, cemented my desire to continue my life in the desert," recalls Gibbs, now a bronze jewelry artist and sculptor. "I was immediately plunged into the residential community at Arcosanti, and welcomed with open arms by the ragtag group of artists and makers that have made their lives here."

It's clear that this settlement is more than just a fanciful architectural experiment in the desert. As it looks to its next 50 years, Arcosanti's significance will take on greater resonance while the world struggles with climate change and the need to reinvent communities as smart cities.

"What any visitor to Arcosanti should take away is the sense that it is not a localized anomaly. It is a testament to the capacity of humankind," says Pappa. "While Arcosanti is often misrepresented as utopian, it is not meant to be idealistic. It is the seed that, when given the right nutrients and care, can be grown in any corner of the world."

"Arcosanti represents a kind of triumph of the imagination."

Soleri had an enduring fascination with domed roofs. In 1949, he helped design a rotating glass roof for a cave-like house cut into the desert north of Phoenix.

In order to grow produce in the desert, the community at Arcosanti harvests
rainwater from the roofs. There is also a gray water system that recycles waste water from sinks and appliances.

Designed by Louis Barthélemy and crafted by Tarek El Safty, these decorative khayamiya marry Egyptian tradition with contemporary art.

*Le cult...
main...*

Khayamiya are used across the Middle East and North Africa to decorate tents for weddings and funerals. However, the appliqué technique is time-consuming and expensive, and has largely been replaced by digital printing. Since they first met three years ago, Barthélemy and El Safty have been working to revive the technique.

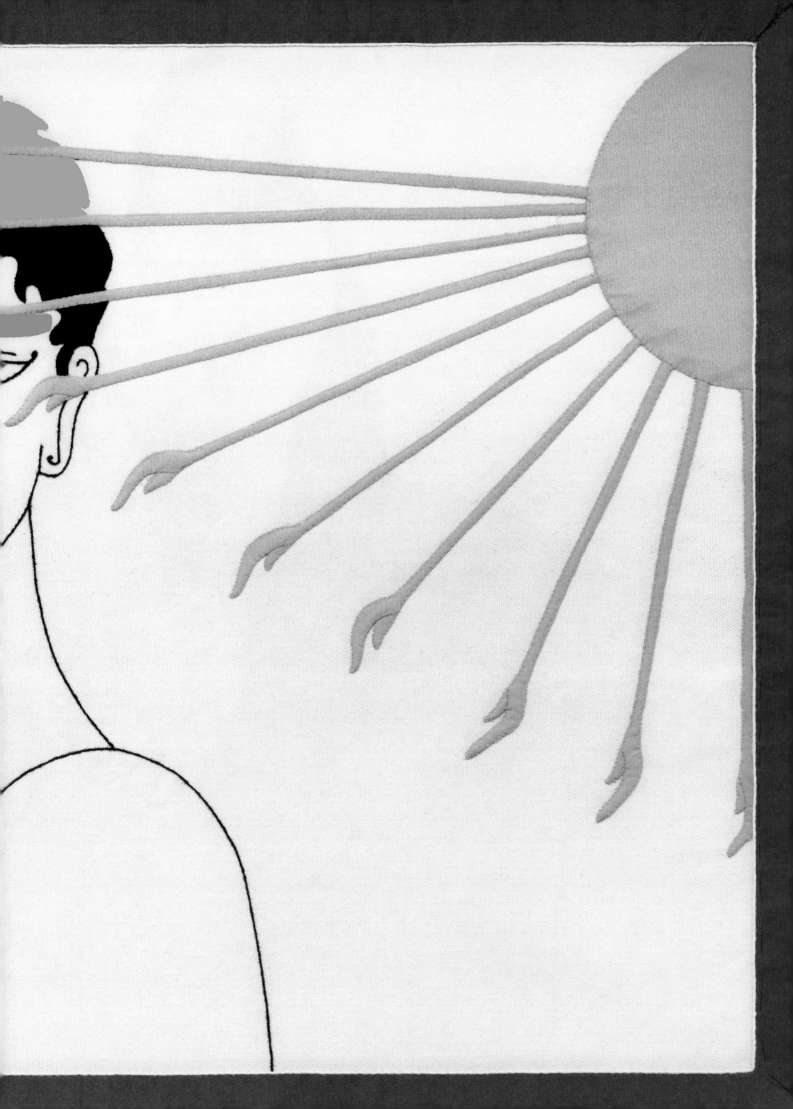

RINA SAWAYAMA:

ELTON JOHN CALLED ME. IT'S *OUT* OF MY IMAGINATION.

Hair: Tomi Roppongi at Saint Luke using Maria Nila, Makeup: Michelle Dacillo using NARS

As pop stars go, Rina Sawayama belongs to the old school. She's a high-energy entertainer with in-your-face melodies, signature dance moves and undeniable glamour. Most often seen in music videos and on stage decked out in futuristic club kid chic, she has an ever-changing array of hair colors to fit her mood. But while Sawayama's music is indulgently sweet and otherworldly, her lyrical content hits much closer to home, tackling consumer culture, racial microaggressions and hereditary trauma.

The singer, now 30, took a relatively slow path to becoming an international pop star. After graduating from Cambridge University with a degree in politics, psychology and sociology in 2012, she worked as a model, appearing in campaigns for the Versus x Versace collection and Mac Cosmetics, while pursuing a career in music. Following the success of the self-released EP *Rina* in 2017, the affable singer-songwriter signed to Dirty Hit and, in 2020, released her debut album, *Sawayama*, a heavy-hitting pop record that veers furiously from nu metal to early noughties R&B and stadium rock.

Her presence in the pop world has already made an impact on the musical landscape. In July 2020,

the British Phonographic Industry announced it will be reviewing the criteria for the Mercury Prize after Sawayama—who was born in Japan and moved to the UK when she was five—kicked off a media storm when she revealed she was not eligible to submit her album as a British artist under the current rules.

SP: *Sawayama is out now. How does it feel to let people into your world?* **RS:** I'm happy because I feel I've made a family album for myself, just the way I wanted it. I like [dividing] it into different scenes; each song is like a scene of a play. As an album it is very varied, but hopefully there's a common thread running throughout.

SP: *Your lyrics cover topics like capitalism, racial microaggressions and climate change. Is it important to you that the listener takes in these messages?* **RS:** The melody has to be amazing, because that's what most people will take with them after the first listen. By thinking about the lyrics a bit more, it gives it a little bit more longevity. I think people want to listen back and perhaps they'll realize things on the eighth listen that they didn't on the first or fifth. It's never really been of interest to me to write a straight-up love song with a heterosexual partner. The things I feel

most passionate about are political things. Two years ago, when I started writing this, I was so knee-deep in climate grief. Right now, there's a lot to be frustrated about as well. I use that as a jumping-off point rather than just, like: "He was a boy, she was a girl."

SP: *You talk a lot on the album about your upbringing, and about your chosen family in the LGBTQ community. What does family mean to you now?* **RS:** I'm actually kind of proud of my family in a weird way. I'm glad I had a really messy family because genuinely I don't think I would have had a lot to talk about otherwise. My first heartbreak probably came from my dad leaving. [Now], my family is constantly evolving. I didn't really come to this idea of a "chosen family" until I met my queer family and they're just as messy as my biological family, but in a different way. I love them so much.

SP: *You now have a large fan base who call themselves "Pixels." How does it feel to have that sort of adoration?* **RS:** It's a really big responsibility, existing online. There's a lot of stuff that goes on behind the scenes I would never want to bring to the fore. Also, there's a lot of "canceling" and a lot of people who say bad stuff about me, but I want to set an example of not canceling people and of

Sawayama wears a dress by 16Arlington, boots by By Far and a hairband by Simone Rocha. Previous spread: She wears a dress by Rejina Pyo.

trying to lead with compassion, education and communication. I didn't see someone like me when I was growing up in pop. There are so few Asians in pop anyway. I don't want to go and fuck it up by just being a messy drama bitch.

SP: *Does it ever feel like a burden?* **RS:** You know, when my mom calls me and she's like, "I don't think you should have said that in interviews," that is when it's a burden. My mom doesn't want her daughter to do anything wrong. The whole tattoos thing, that already gives her so much anxiety and stress. I guess I try not to think about it too much. Seeing Asian people who aren't happy with what I'm doing, or queer people who might not be happy with what I'm saying, that's hurtful, but at the same time, my biggest thing is I want to reach as many people as possible because that's what representation is.

SP: *There are a lot of early noughties influences on your latest album. Are these musical choices driven by nostalgia?* **RS:** I never intend for something to sound a certain way; I always let the melody and the lyrics dictate the production. That's why this record ended up so eclectic—each song had its own little personality that needed to be drawn out in a different way. If I was set on having my own version of nostalgia I wouldn't have a song like "Who's Gonna Save U Now" on the record, or "Dynasty."

SP: *What inspires your visual aesthetic?* **RS:** I just wanted to look like a weird creature, but it's also very, very Asian. My glam team [for *Sawayama*] was all Asian so we're coming with authentic references and pushing it into that, like, sci-fi or fantasy world. I'm super proud of the cover art. I look very yellow, which I really love. Almost gilded or golden.

SP: *I was trying to place you in this era of British pop and I'm not sure where exactly you fit. What do you see for yourself in the future?* **RS:** I wish I could be like, "I'm gonna be the next Lady Gaga." I just want to do my best and see where it goes. But I did my best and this album went so much better than I ever would have imagined. Like, Elton John called me. He just called me from his house phone to say that he saw an article about me. That's so wildly out of my imagination, so if things like that keep happening that'd be cool.

Sawayama wears a top by Toga Archives, trousers by A.W.A.K.E. Mode, heels by By Far and earrings by Maria Black.

Below: Sawayama wears an outfit by Toga Archives and earrings by Maria Black. Right: She wears a dress by 16Arlington.

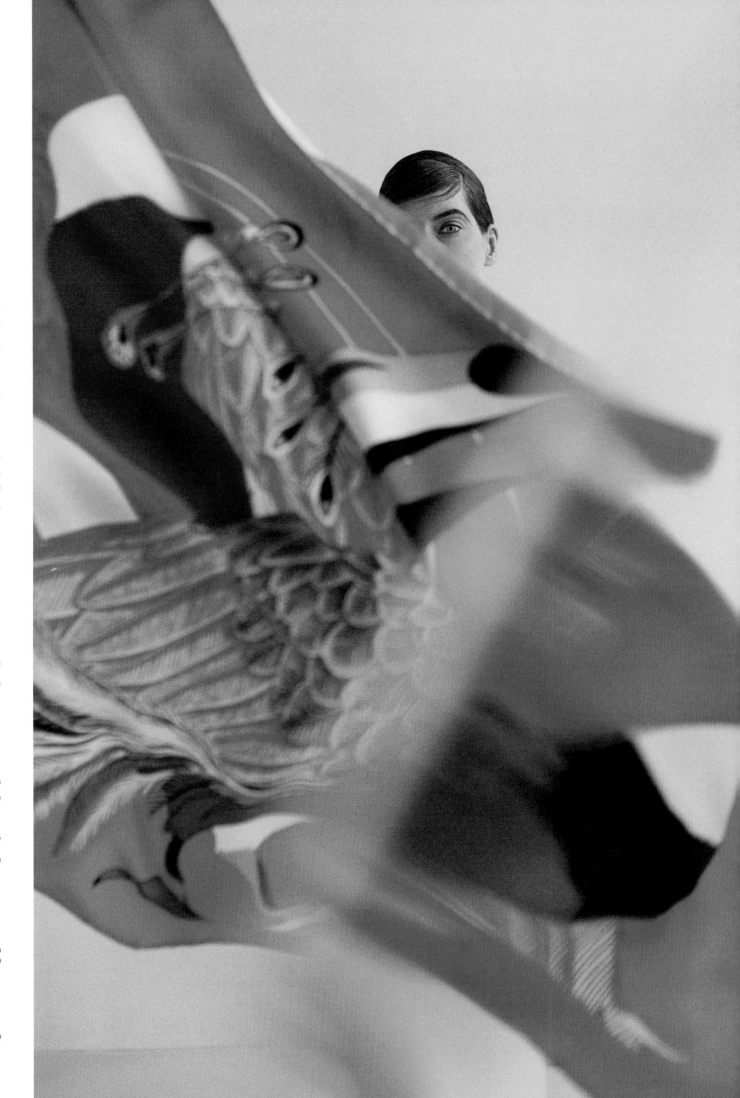

Through the looking glass, a landscape of strange possibilities and proportions lies in wait. Photography by Pelle Crépin @ Styling by Katy Lassen

UNDER
THE ILLUSION

Jasmijn wears a coat by MM6 Maison Margiela and trousers by Rejina Pyo. Previous: She wears a skirt by Live the Process and waves a scarf by Hermès.

Above: Jasmijn wears a top by Roksanda, a coat by Joseph and earrings by Completedworks. Right: She wears a dress by Roksanda.

Above: Jasmijn wears a dress by Issey Miyake and a hat by Roksanda. Right: She wears a top by Hermès and trousers by MM6 Maison Margiela. Lipstick by Hermès.

Left: Jasmijn wears a top by Preen by Thornton Bregazzi and trousers by MM6 Maison Margiela. Above: She wears a dress by Chalayan and shoes by Rejina Pyo.

Jasmijn wears a dress by Christopher Kane.

At Work With:
Green River Project

Aaron Aujla and *Ben Bloomstein* switched lanes from art to design, and found their true calling as outsiders in the world of interiors. Words by *Cody Delistraty* & Photography by *Dominik Tarabański*

To a certain sort of Brooklynite, Ben Bloomstein and Aaron Aujla's Green River Project might feel like it's been around forever. Working mostly from a studio in Hillsdale, New York, where Bloomstein's family owns a farm, they've crafted conceptual, sculptural furniture that's without frills: chairs, tables, cabinets, stools, dining sets, sofas and more made from raw materials like unvarnished pine and black hyedua wood. Their materials tend also to be shot through with personal references, like lumber taken from the titular Green River, for instance, or jute and bamboo that reflects Aujla's Indian heritage. Their clients include tastemakers like Mirabelle Marden and Mary-Kate and Ashley Olsen's The Row. Add to that the fact that they also have a wood shop in the Bedford-Stuyvesant neighborhood of Brooklyn as well as their brick-and-mortar storefront in Manhattan's East Village, and it comes as something of a surprise to learn that they only incorporated Green River Project as a business three years ago, in the fall of 2017.

But as quickly as Green River Project became a staple of the design, fashion and furniture worlds, there was nearly a decade of preparation to establish its foundations. Aujla, who grew up in British Columbia, Canada, and studied art history and fine art at the University of Toronto, had been working as an assistant to a painter while trying to become a painter himself. Bloomstein, who grew up in upstate New York, had been an art handler while woodworking on the side. Aujla, in particular, had been looking to take his art practice to the next level. Even though Bloomstein was a bit reluctant at first, they decided to join forces. "We'd had all of these conversations and similarities before we ever started," says Aujla. "We already spoke the same language."

Inspired by Aujla's fiancée, Emily Bode, who won last year's CFDA Emerging Designer of the Year award for her handmade clothing, Green River Project began releasing their furniture collections quarterly, in line with the international fashion calendar—a decision that's helped keep them in the forefront of conversations surrounding both fashion and design. *Kinfolk* spoke with Bloomstein and Aujla about their friendship, their early aesthetic and how they bring their own personalities and backgrounds to bear on furniture design.

CD: *How did your collaboration begin?* **AA:** I waited for Ben forever. I was working with Clarion Gallery in New York and Brussels, and, as a painter, I was reaching a standstill. [I was] disgruntled with the way that the art world worked, and the way young, emerging artists were packaged and sold. Ben was happier to experiment a little while. But I was ready to move on. I wanted to do interiors, but I knew that I wouldn't have done interiors or furniture without Ben, so I was waiting for him to be at the right time in his life to make a transition. **BB:** I wasn't ready to throw in the towel, so to speak, or throw it in for a new towel. I wasn't necessarily as gung ho about it in the beginning. I was happy with where I was at. And I didn't actually believe that it would work, because I felt no one would really take us seriously.

Design dealer Michael Bargo, interviewed on page 183, gave Green River Project the keys to an elite strata of the design sphere when he exhibited its inaugural collection at New York's Collective Design fair in 2017.

FEATURES

CD: *Why didn't you think you'd be taken seriously?* **BB:** Because we weren't coming from a design background. We didn't really know any interior designers or architects. We didn't know the industry at all. Maybe that's part of why we were successful. That's something Aaron saw that I didn't see. There was a space in that industry for us that people didn't even know they were missing.

CD: *You have a few staple pieces, like the One Pine-Board Chair. How did you initially conceive of Green River's aesthetic?* **AA:** The first time I met Ben I realized I'd met someone very different from other people. He has his own philosophy of the way he lives, down to eating and dressing. It was really taking the things that Ben enjoyed making for whatever reason. That chair was about economy of material and a game with yourself. How do we make a chair out of a board? Everything starts with some sort of idea like that. We were also really interested in photographs becoming part of the narrative. That's why we use Andrew Jacobs. He's the only person we've ever used to shoot our furniture, and I got him from my fiancée, Emily Bode, who was using him for her clothing. From the beginning, we were really interested in controlling every end of making furniture. **BB:** One of the reasons we work well together is the fact that we're control freaks but in different ways. Especially in the beginning, we talked about what was missing from each of our homes. Green River ultimately was a tool to gain control. We weren't buying it from someone else or another builder or designer or being at a store's mercy. Whenever we butt heads in the process, where we might not see eye to eye, it becomes an interesting interplay of our individual needs to control things. That's actually when the best work happens.

CD: *What are the tensions in your relationship? How does that play out in your designs?* **AA:** We've found it really easy to work together. Even recently, it almost just gets easier and easier because you know what the other person's going to bring to the table. But Ben, sometimes he's extra crazy. Sometimes he'll draw things, and I'll be like, "I have no idea how anyone is going to incorporate that into their home. Is that a hardware collection? How do we even price that thing?"

CD: *What's an example? That's pretty funny.* **AA:** Man, there are so many examples. Once Ben drew a table that was supposed to be a road and the sconces above were like cars on a highway. I remember saying, This is just totally ridiculous. But Ben was like, I'm going to make it for my home. **BB:** Aaron will either be like, "Yeah, man, I think that that would be really cool for '21 or '22," which is code for "This needs a lot of work and time and you're going to have to come back to this." If it's closer, he'll be like, "Yeah, this is cool, let's take another pass at it and try again," and then usually that's when Aaron and I will work together. We end up making the same thing over and over and over again, getting closer and closer. We do draw things, but we don't necessarily make detailed drawings before we produce something. Unless it's for a client, we make a simple sketch without even dimensions and then just start.

CD: *What's the emotional through line of your work?* **AA:** A lot of times using your own biographical jumping-off point is a way to remind yourself to make something that's truthful. It's hard to think about making anything these days without either historical references or contemporary references. My family's from Punjab, and the bamboo furniture, for example, has to do with the Indian craft of using jute and bamboo to

hold together a chair or piece of furniture. That whole collection, even the tones and the colors, came directly from fabrics and things that I collected traveling. The collection about Ben's grandfather and the metalwork and the welding jackets—or even making a piece of clothing and draping it over a chair—is really an expression of Ben. **BB:** In the first few collections, it was really clear where the references were coming from, whether it was from Aaron's history or my own. As we've made more collections, we talk about it a little bit less. But it's an unspoken subtext to everything that we make. We've developed a language and the language is based on our own histories and our own experiences.

CD: *What's next?* **BB:** Even before quarantine, the plan for 2020 has always been to go back to our roots. Down the road from where we started is where Ellsworth Kelly's studio was for the last 20, 30 years of his life, and the river, the Green River, starts in this town called Spencertown and then slows down along the New York and Massachusetts border where my family's land is and where the barn that we started Green River is. We have been harvesting wood from the banks of the river for two years. Now all that lumber is dried and cured and ready to be built into furniture. We're going to be using Ellsworth Kelly shapes and some of his reliefs as a starting-off point for the shape and then obviously the wood is a reference to the area and the river. The idea has always been that when someone buys a chair or a credenza or whatever, rather than the lumber just coming from any old supplier, we prefer if the lumber came from a special place so we could maintain that control of the material from start to finish—so we can add that history into every piece of furniture until this lumber runs out. It's further end-to-end control. It's not just control, it's also about a history instilled into the material.

"We didn't know the industry at all. Maybe that's part of why we were successful."

Essay:

Social Work

Words by Hettie O'Brien

Advice for separating work and home life focuses on the physical: Don't work in bed, take lunch away from your desk. But what about our online lives? For people working in the creative industries, where jobs are scarce and technology ubiquitous, the desire to switch off is often outweighed by the pressure to be "always on"—always commenting, connecting and maintaining a lifestyle that accords with the aspirations of any given industry. On the back of a global lockdown that blurred the work-life barrier like never before, Hettie O'Brien considers the cost of never logging off.

Would anyone's utopia have social media? Not mine. Twitter would never have been invented. (But everyone would have a permanent contract, parental leave and a spacious apartment.) In real life, however, having an online presence has become a means of attaining these things, a requisite for demonstrating your employability, a way of surmounting gatekeepers to enter industries without familial connections. Everyone understands the bad parts of social media: that it quantifies social status and assigns us all a score; that it collapses the border between private lives and professional selves, serving up both for the disenchantment of anonymous others. But what about the good: Is it even funny, or clever? Does mastering the form indicate anything beyond the form itself? Who knows.

What I do know is that this compulsion does not apply equally: Those doing socially useful labor, such as stocking supermarket shelves or caring for children, are not required to be online. But for a small minority of the workforce— those people chasing employment that confers social prestige in industries where job opportunities are scarce and digital technologies ubiquitous—the demand of being "always on" is inextricably and inevitably tied up with work.

One of the great ironies of human ingenuity is how technologies invented to save time in fact created more work. In her classic history *More Work for Mother*, Ruth Schwartz Cowan demonstrated that, instead of reducing domestic labor and traditional "women's work," inventions like the vacuum cleaner and washing machine redirected and even intensified it.[1] Though these modern conveniences extended middle-class comforts to working-class women and housewives, by increasing the volume of work it was possible to complete in a day, and by prescribing new standards of cleanliness, they both extended and augmented the burden of domestic labor. The relationship between social media and work is similar. It's not that social media has stopped us from being productive—stroking your phone while awaiting the next dopamine hit is perfectly consonant with holding down a job and a meaningful social life— rather, it's that the expectation of being always available has both altered and prolonged the work we are expected to do.

"There's a common feeling among employees today that it's not enough to fulfill the tasks that have been circumscribed for you," Josh Cohen, the psychoanalyst and author of *Not Working*, a book that criticizes our culture of overwork and lauds the benefits of idleness, tells me. "To be properly productive, and to be seen to be properly productive, you always have to be going a bit beyond what's asked of you." This pressure suffuses our jobs and the extracurricular enterprises that we feel "benignly railroaded into participating in, in order to increase [our] presence and profile," Cohen explains, "whether it's the podcast, the blog, the Twitter feed, the 'side hustle.'"

Many employees and freelancers in industries where jobs are short-term or shrinking feel that it's no longer *enough* to just do their work, and that it's now incumbent upon them to tend professional profiles on multiple platforms, always looking for the next opportunity. "There is a kind of shame about dropping out, about saying you won't be available online or on email," Cohen says. "I wonder why a lot of my colleagues bother with out-of-office notices—they never seem to be out of office."

This sense that we have to *be* our jobs, to divulge some deeper substrate of our selfhood in order to get ahead in the marketplace, is partly explained by economic shifts that have occurred over the last 40 years. From the 1980s onward, businesses began to offshore and downsize to reduce labor costs and chase profits. The result was an upsurge in outsourcing, and short-term or freelance contracts. Workers in this new economy have been forced to adapt to a life where jobs are fleeting and spending time as "independent contractors" is normal. At the same time, digital technologies such as email entered the workplace, allowing employers to indirectly monitor productivity and prolong working hours.[2] The effects of these changes were both social and psychological: Workers are now expected to be flexible, entrepreneurial, reactive—and to demand less from the safety nets once offered by permanent employment.

In our new marketplace of short-term work, where online followings can be leveraged to secure employment opportunities, the distinction between personal and professional selfhood has become porous. In a blog post published during lockdown, Hussein Kesvani, author of *Follow Me, Akhi: The Online World of British Muslims*, wrote that "at a time when my generation have less access to the milestones of personal development, where ownership is a luxury... there are few things more reassuring than numbers. The numbers on our Twitter accounts and Instagram pictures."

This technocratic, numerical evaluation of professional relevance and digital popularity can bleed into the way we approach relationships with other humans. "When your means of survival are partly dependent on you making connections online, you're required to invest emotional energy into transactional kinds of relationships—on the basis that if you become good friends with a person, it could turn into a job later on," Kesvani tells me.

The anxieties associated with integrating personal and professional identity recur in Cohen's psychotherapy practice: "The more energy and anxiety

---

NOTES

1. Cowan noted that, by 1950, an American housewife could singlehandedly do the same amount of household labor as a staff of three or four in 1850.
—
—
—

2. About 50% of large companies had remote monitoring techniques in place by 2018, including surveying social media usage or reading messages on Slack. One recent survey anticipated that 80% would be using these techniques by the end of 2020.

3. According to a report by the US National Bureau of Economic Research published in July 2020, the average American workday was 48 minutes longer during lockdown than prior to it.
—
—

"Perhaps the idea of logging off presupposes that, at some profound level, we're not really like this; that there is a possible world where we could be happier, less transactional, more guarded of our inner lives."

we're investing into cultivating our public external profiles, the less we expend on the cultivation of our private lives," he explains. Lifting the curtain on the production of digital identity reveals a spectacle that is often narcissistic, vulnerable and politically expressive in all the wrong ways. There's something—forgive me—so *embarrassing* about it all, this compulsion to perform one's professional credentials for the accretion of numbers that indicate nothing more than elusive notions of "engagement" and "influence."

It would be convenient to assume the answer lies in simply exiting the "virtual" world and logging off from the pressures it prescribes. But to assume that online and offline selfhood can be easily disaggregated is, regrettably, a fiction—particularly when the pandemic has dictated an unprecedented experiment in working from home, where remote employees are expected to be more online than ever before and Slack channels and virtual meetings have outmoded face-to-face contact. (Research shows that these workers—armed with all of the conveniences of digital technology—have, like housewives with microwaves, begun to work paradoxically longer hours.)[3]

Two questions I return to often are: What's it all for? and When can I log off? Perhaps the idea of logging off presupposes that, at some profound level, we're not really like this; that there is a possible world where we could be happier, less transactional, more guarded of our inner lives. But there is no realer real than the reality that most of us participate in, where the pressures of digital selfhood are internalized.

"Saying to somebody in therapy that you don't want to hear about their social media field is incredibly naive and disingenuous," Cohen says. "The public gaze, and the sense of forever being heard and seen in its presence and absence, is so much a part of their self-understanding." When I ask Kesvani about logging off, he tells me that he often thinks about what being online would be like without its concomitant pressures of self-improvement and professional identification. "I was thinking to myself the other day," he said: "When was the last time I had fun?"

From 50 fathoms under, Jacques Cousteau taught a generation to love the

oceans. But as Annick Weber learns, the maritime explorer's own ambitions and

preoccupations always swam close to the surface.

JC

In the autumn of 1977, Jacques Cousteau was on a six-week tour of the US to raise funds for filming his much-loved documentary series that was airing on American television at the time. The lectures sold out in each city he visited, attracting crowds bigger than many rock bands. During a stop in Seattle, a group of local schoolchildren came to meet him before the event. Handing him a drawing of a colorful underwater world, one child shyly asked what it was really like deep down in the sea. "It's fantastic underwater," Cousteau answered with a dazzling smile. "It feels like floating in space."

With his red hat, long wiry face and instantly recognizable French accent, the then 67-year-old oceanographer had become a subject of fascination the world over for opening humans up to a previously unknown part of the planet: oceans. Sailing around the world on the Calypso, his ship and floating lab, Cousteau dedicated his life to exploring the sea and all forms of underwater life, and shared his adventures with millions of television viewers in hit series such as *The Undersea World of Jacques Cousteau* and *The Cousteau Odyssey*. "He was an extremely charismatic person and a master showman: He knew how to explain the ocean environment to people in ways that didn't necessarily involve hard science," Brad Matsen, the author of the biography *Jacques Cousteau: The Sea King*, tells me on the phone. "We knew so little about it that the idea of him roaming around and filming underwater was immediately attractive. He showed us places we could only imagine going."

Funnily enough, despite his contagious, almost childlike enthusiasm, being a maritime explorer never figured in the young Cousteau's dreams. Born to an upper-middle-class family near Bordeaux in 1910, he had three career ambitions as a boy: to become a pilot, a film director, or a medical doctor. Though he learned to dive before his 10th birthday, he was determined to pursue the goals he had set out, saving up his pocket money to buy an early Pathé movie camera at age 13 and later entering the École Navale to train in naval aviation. But his life changed its course drastically when one foggy evening he crashed his father's sports car and broke both his arms. The accident forced Cousteau to rethink his professional choice of flying airplanes, and so he turned to the ocean instead, starting to shoot underwater films with his friends from naval college in the early 1940s and experimenting with breathing equipment to be able to dive for longer.

If Cousteau is today known for having co-invented, among others, the Aqua-Lung scuba regulator, the world probably owes the contraptions he came up with to his insatiable quest for the best footage. "As madcap as they may seem, the inventions of Cousteau were in fact extremely pragmatic," Matsen explains. "He created the Aqua-Lung because he wanted to make [his 1943 film] *Épaves*. The first ocean dive he did with its prototype was to harvest lobster. He was an opportunist; he was driven not so much by his advocacy of science, but by his desire to do exactly what he wanted to do." For example, when World War II prevented him from finding blank reels of film for making *Épaves*, he ended up splicing together hundreds of small reels designed for a brand of children's camera.

In *The Undersea World of Jacques Cousteau*, the explorer uses inventive and often foolhardy techniques to film animals in close proximity, including approaching hippos by hiding inside a hippo-shaped stalking horse.

"The sea's most monstrous force doesn't live in Loch Ness. It lives in us."

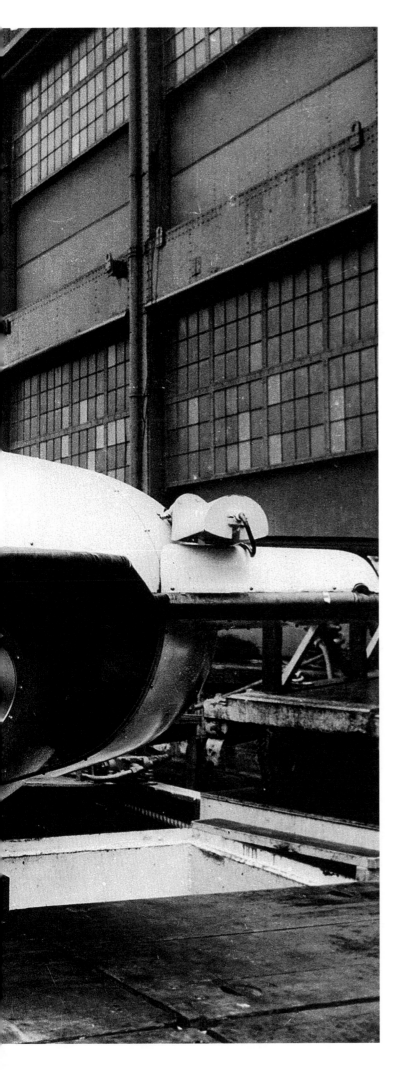

> *"Man has only to sink beneath the surface and he is free. Under water, man becomes an archangel."*

Later, for his 1956 documentary *The Silent World*—which won the Palme d'Or and an Academy Award—he shot over 15 miles of film, of which only one-tenth were used in the final version.

In everything he did, Cousteau was guided by his unquenchable curiosity. Since floating underwater was the closest he could get to his childhood dream of flying, he pushed boundaries to chase the freedom of the deep sea and capture it for generations to come.

Cousteau once wrote: "From birth, man carries the weight of gravity on his shoulders. He is bolted to the Earth. But man has only to sink beneath the surface and he is free. Buoyed by water, he can fly in any direction—up, down, sideways—by merely flipping his hand. Under water, man becomes an archangel."

To keep pursuing his passion, he thought outside existing systems. In the 1960s, Cousteau and his team built a series of pressurized underwater habitats in which they could live and work directly on the seafloor. Large windows with unblocked views of the real-life aquarium enabled them to study the ocean environment in more depth. When the crew reappeared after 30 days continuously spent underwater, they had set a new world record that only Cousteau's grandson, the aquanaut Fabien Cousteau, would break 51 years later.

While the first half of Cousteau's life was dominated by exploring and filming the undersea world, he would spend the years until his death in 1997 advocating for its preservation. Over four decades of expeditions, he began to notice that this once rich and biodiverse realm was becoming the victim of pollution. The waters of his youth were increasingly robbed of their crystalline quality by heavy metals and other toxins, leading him to conclude that "the sea's most monstrous force doesn't live in Loch Ness. It lives in us."

To educate people about the alarming state of the oceans, he founded the still-active Cousteau Society in 1973. Around that time, he also started dedicating entire episodes of *The Cousteau Odyssey* television series to environmental disaster, contrasting old footage of colorful marine life with shots of today's bleak reality. "The concept of ecology simply didn't exist in most households until Cousteau came on television," Matsen insists. "People started to understand that we have got to change our ways or otherwise we will extinguish ourselves. He surely wasn't the first to popularize the environmental movement, but he was its first mass hero."

Despite uncovering more of the underwater world than anyone before him, Cousteau remained an outsider to the scientific establishment. While some oceanographers doubted the importance of his research, others accused him of hypocrisy, especially when it came to his ecological commitments. They questioned how someone who had his first missions sponsored by the likes of British Petroleum could suddenly be a champion of marine conservation. Many also accused him of capturing dolphins to get the best wildlife shots for his films. To Cousteau's admirers, however, he was aware of his own failings and his preservation efforts were an honest attempt to reverse some of the ills he had committed in the 1950s.

What matters today is that his work not only laid the foundation for generations' worth of research, but shared the importance of protecting the oceans with the world. "We owe a lot of our dreams and our sense of curiosity to him," Fabien Cousteau says of his grandfather's legacy. "His work inspired people to make better decisions in their daily lives, so that hopefully, in the future, we can live with the ocean as our life support system, rather than eating away at it."

Left Photograph: Popperfoto/Getty Image. Overleaf: Photograph: © AGIP / Bridgeman Images

3.

Rituals

114 — 176

In Seoul, the ancient art of tattoo is thrown into sharp relief. Photography by Giseok Cho & Styling by Yeon You

NEEDLE WORK

Above: Sungsik wears a skirt by Kimhekim. Right: Miki wears a dress by Sun Woo.

Left: Miki wears a dress by Sun Woo. Below: Sungsik wears a top by Leje.

Above: Miki wears a dress by Tchai Kim and Sungsik wears trousers by Kimhekim. Right: Miki wears a dress by Sun Woo.

ABBY STEIN: I WANTED TO BE AN *EDUCATED* REBEL.

Above: Stein wears a jacket
by Bally. Right: She wears a blazer
by Christian Wijnants and trousers
by The Break. Previous: She wears a
dress by Vaquera and a turtleneck
by The Break.

Rabbi Abby Stein speaks to *Unorthodox* author *Deborah Feldman* about her gender transition, her relationship to tradition and her departure from the ultra-Orthodox community they both grew up in. Photography by *Katie McCurdy* & Styling by *Dominick Barcelona*

Set Design: Javier Irigoyen, Hair: Dana Boyer, Makeup: Katie Mellinger

At 29, Abby Stein occupies a unique position: She is the first publicly transgender woman to have grown up in the ultra-Orthodox Hasidic Jewish community. Today, the Columbia graduate is a speaker, activist and the author of *Becoming Eve: My Journey From Ultra-Orthodox Rabbi to Transgender Woman*. But getting to this point has taken incalculable grit. Stein grew up in a prestigious, rabbinical family in an enclave of Williamsburg that felt more like a 19th-century Eastern European shtetl than Brooklyn, New York. She spoke no English until she was 20, had no access to the internet, and was confined to male roles in a society with some of the most rigid gender segregation policies in the world.

When Stein left the community in 2012, one of the first books she read was Deborah Feldman's memoir, *Unorthodox: The Scandalous Rejection of My Hasidic Roots*, published earlier that year, which charted Feldman's own departure from the same community and neighborhood. It has recently found a global audience with its Netflix adaptation. Over Zoom, Feldman interviewed Stein about their shared path, Stein's current relationship to her faith and its rituals, and her recent return to working as a rabbi. "I started missing the fun part," says Stein. "It was about the foods, the music, the community. I think it took me a while to get to a point of being okay with that."

DF: *We've spoken briefly as part of a panel discussion, and you appeared as a background character in* Unorthodox *on Netflix, but there are a lot of things I still don't know. Tell me about how your process of leaving began.* **AS:** The first Sabbath that I broke a prohibition was directly after my son's circumcision, in January 2012. I couldn't read or communicate well in English then, but I started perusing Hebrew-language forums; I remember a page on which they were talking about trans people. Those first few months were actually really hard, and I remember thinking I wish someone could help me. Then someone added me to the Ex-Orthodox Facebook group, which had only 200 members at the time. That's when I started meeting people. And then shortly after I had a long conversation with my wife—but about religion, not about gender. I was sure she was going to leave me. It got to a point on the eve of the Jewish New Year in 2012 where her parents told her that she had to leave me. And she said no. Which was really impressive.

NOTES

1. *Unorthodox: The Scandalous Rejection of My Hasidic Roots* is a 2012 memoir by Deborah Feldman that documents the author's childhood in the Satmar sect of Brooklyn's Jewish community, her escape from an arranged marriage at the age of 19 while pregnant with her first child, and how she eventually resettled in Germany.

2. Footsteps, a New York-based non-profit organization, provides people wishing to leave a Haredi or Hasidic Jewish community with social and emotional support services, plus educational and vocational guidance. Footsteps states it has served over 1,700 people since its founding in 2003.

"By the time you realize who you are, you have five kids, you're stuck in the community, you have no skills to help you leave."

DF: *Definitely impressive. What happened next?* **AS:** Our family is a rabbinical [the Hasidic equivalent of nobllity] family, so the rebbe [supreme spiritual leader] agreed to speak to my wife, even though he normally doesn't speak to women, as her family was hoping he would convince her to leave me. However, he just gave me a set of conditions for the continuation of the marriage. For example, he told me I'm not allowed to go to the library, which is so 1930s! When he was a teenager in Romania, that's where all the rebel kids went. Instead I needed to pray every day, etcetera. Eventually I confessed to my wife that I had no interest in remaining Orthodox, but was willing to make certain compromises. More and more people were accusing me of heresy. Then my wife's mother showed up and announced she was taking her daughter home. And after this my wife disappeared from my life. I don't actually know what happened to her exactly. We never had that last conversation.

DF: *What about the connection with your son? For me, so much of leaving was bound up with promising my son a better life. So few women manage to leave the community with their children, despite their best efforts, and I don't even know of men who have attempted to do so. That is one of the most painful aspects of leaving for many—that complete break in contact with one's children.* **AS:** At first, they shut me out for a few weeks. They didn't let me see my son at all; they clearly wanted to get full custody and to ensure that I shouldn't have any relationship with him—but of course they needed a *get* [a religious divorce].

DF: *Right, in the Jewish tradition only the husband can grant the divorce.* **AS:** So I said, "Listen, if she wants a *get* we're doing a *get* tomorrow, but I'm in no rush. I don't care. I don't need it."

DF: *That's some really good leverage in terms of ensuring contact with your son. It's power I didn't have when I left, which is why the battle dragged on for so many years in my case. And why I needed my book—it was integral in custody negotiations.* **AS:** They wanted a *get* super fast. I didn't know at the time why, but it turns out she had secretly become engaged. They were afraid for her soul. And so they started pushing and I said, "Sure, we'll do a normal joint custody agreement." They were a bit resistant, but essentially they had no choice.

I squeezed some clever clauses into the agreement, for example that they couldn't control how I dressed during visitation with my son. They were in such a rush at the time they just thought it meant not being dressed Hasidic. I was very much aware already that it meant more. So I got a really good custody agreement, and the second we were divorced, I had nothing else keeping me in the Hasidic community.

DF: *Do you think there is any introspection happening within these communities about why people are leaving?* **AS:** My dad told me the way to deal with "weak youth" was to marry them off at 18 and then they'd be stuck. He said this openly. This isn't just something that happens casually as a result of tradition, it is an intentional strategy. I was reading this psychological study once about how most people only fully develop their brains at age 25. So by the time you realize who you are, you are doomed. You have five kids, you're stuck in the community, you have no skills to help you leave.

DF: *There seems to be a new policy throughout, that the community can no longer shut people off who leave, because there are simply too many.* **AS:** There used to be shame involved. Now it's like every extended family has kids that have left.

DF: *We both agree that this wouldn't have been the case 10 years ago, right? People aren't getting shut out in quite the same way when they leave.* **AS:** Yeah. I think what is happening is that the shame is gone. They are realizing that there's nothing to gain—like my father said, if you stay close, maybe they will come back. My family stayed in touch with me even after I started college, until I came out. Then the shame came back all over again. Because I was the first trans person. And then they really did stop talking to me.

DF: *You know, I'm obsessed with this figure who repeatedly crops up in Yiddish cultural narratives based on the Ludmirer moyd [maiden of Ludmir], the only woman in Hasidism to become a rebbe [spiritual leader]. But we don't have an opposite role model because at least in Orthodox Judaism, things are set up so that the man is on a higher rung than the woman. And in order to achieve this higher rung of spirituality, of closeness to God, the woman has no choice but to become a man. Whereas I imagine that Judaism would see the reverse transition as a move away from God. And so I'm asking myself if the community sees trans men and trans women differently.* **AS:** Well, my dad definitely did. I started my physical transition in September 2015. I had already come out to my super-hip progressive rabbi months before I came out publicly, and he had said to me he wanted to be there when I came out to my father.

He had grown up Orthodox as well and he had developed a relationship with my father already. My dad would try to debate him all the time.

I think my dad was convinced I was gay. My mom just didn't know what to make of it. But they were always concerned that something was going on. They didn't know that trans people exist.

Right: Stein wears a blazer by Christian Wijnants and trousers by The Break.
Below: She wears a shirt by Bode and a hat by Edas. Previous spread: She wears head-to-toe Bally.

DF: *But this stuff is discussed in the Talmud, right? It's not a secret.* **AS:** I remember asking in yeshiva [a form of religious school] about how the Talmud says there are at least six genders. And the answer was always, "Oh, they used to exist in the time of the Temple, but they don't exist anymore"—which is always the go-to answer by the way! Or that it's metaphorical: "It's about the soul, it's not about real life." That was also a favored explanation.

Since I was a teenager, my dad would tell me he knew I was hiding something, and he wasn't wrong. I had an affair with a boy that lasted two years, which, quite frankly, was one of my longest relationships. Obviously, none of us had any sex ed at all. But we figured stuff out.

So in November 2015 I called up my dad and said, "You remember you were always trying to get me to tell you what's going on? I'm ready to tell you. Would you come meet with the rabbi?" I wanted to talk from an emotional level. But the rabbi was smart, he said, "No, we need to approach this from the spiritual perspective."

DF: *Yeah, that makes sense—use his language.* **AS:** We did. We found some really interesting texts, like a quote from the 18th-century Hasidic Rebbe Michel of Zlotchov, which claims that at times a female will be reincarnated in a male body. And we're direct descendants of his, so my dad couldn't just dismiss it. The rabbi and I tried to explain my transition to him using these spiritual concepts, even though to me it's about identity and biology, but that was the only framework he could grasp. After an hour I could see in his eyes that it had clicked, and he said, "Yes, it is theoretically possible, but only a zaddik [the Jewish equivalent of a saint, a righteous one] can know this for sure." So he is saying, he will only accept this when an authority that he trusts confirms it.

DF: *You know how the men wear the gartl [a knit sash worn during prayer] to separate the body into physical and spiritual sections? Women don't wear it because they are considered all physical. When I was growing up it was always explained to me that a man is spirituality and a woman is physicality. The man connects to God and the woman takes care of everything so the man can connect to God and she connects through him—using his line, so to speak. So is your father perhaps looking at this as a kind of distancing from spirituality? As if by entering the female experience, you become estranged from God?*

AS: He turned to me then and, abandoning the religious metaphors, he switched to Yiddish, excluding the rabbi from our conversation, and asked, "Why would you do this? Women are so much less than men." He said this in a confiding way, like, Between me and you, we know the truth, no matter what stories we tell to make women feel better. Which I also found crazy because I had spent an hour pouring my heart out to him. I had told him that when I was three and four years old, I used to try to cut my penis off.

DF: Abby, remember when *Unorthodox* appeared and all these Hasidic people wrote op-eds saying, "This is a disgusting lie, obviously for us a woman is the most important thing." They show you proof in the texts, pointing to places where it says that a woman's pleasure is paramount. **AS:** *It's not reality!*

DF: *We study the text, we say the text is the ultimate authority and yet every single day we flout authority?* **AS:** They are not a religion. That's why I call them a culture or a *culture*. Their biggest issue is cultural. If you don't dress a certain way, if you don't speak a certain way—this has nothing to do with religion.

DF: *I found this very traumatic as a child, to have to deal with such contradictions.* **AS:** There's no doubt it's traumatic. The only way I stayed sane was by leaning into some of these texts.

DF: *How do you mean "leaning into"?* **AS:** Like when I studied *Sha'ar Ha'gilgulim [Doors of Reincarnation]* when I was 16, and I read about transgender reincarnations. I was very much aware that if I took this text to my dad and said, "Hey, this is who I am," he's not gonna care, he's not going to accept it. There's this disconnect.

DF: *So did you feel like you could leave your community and your family without having to reject the texts?* **AS:** Well, I do reject the text. I don't see it as divine. I'm not that kind of believer. I always tell people, if they ask me if I believe in God, "You have to define what belief means and what God means." But if you think about the God that we grew up with, which I call the bogeyman in the sky… well. I like a lot of messages in Hasidic Judaism, or in Judaism as a whole. I don't just see it as okay for me to pick and choose; I think this is what Jews have been doing throughout history. And I think that is beautiful. Like, specifically in non-Orthodox communities they talk about how it's a Jewish thing to ask questions. I was kind of told that as a child as well, but it wasn't really accurate in reality.

DF: *Well, they told us that women cannot study the Torah because God created women to ask too many questions.* **AS:** Maybe that's why I was asking so many questions.

DF: *What's your relationship with religion like now?* **AS:** Well, I got ordained, so technically I have a legit, accredited rabbinical degree. Since I'm legally a female, this also makes me the first accredited female Hasidic rabbi. The degree is not easy to get, it takes five years, but a big part of me wanted to know what I was rebelling against. I wanted to be an educated rebel.

DF: *Do you perform the duties of a rabbi?* **AS:** At first I didn't want to have anything to do with it. Then I started realizing, I'm good at it. I also realized that it has a lot of power, in a good way, in progressive circles. I always tell people, "I couldn't care less why you do or don't observe, but I do care that a lot of people who want to be part of communities should be able to find spiritual communities." I still feel itchy when someone says "Rabbi Abby Stein," but I use it as a description, rather than a title. I feel a bit more comfortable with that. It's evolving. I think we were always told that there's one truth and like life is immutable and nothing changes. I'm very much of the belief that everything's always in flux. The day I figure out everything in life, then what's the point?

Left: Stein wears a dress by Vaquera and a turtleneck by The Break.

Essay:

It's All Greek

Words by Stephanie d'Arc Taylor

Since the first fraternity was founded in 1825, American college life has come to be defined by networks of rituals, secret codes and internal hierarchies whose influences stretch far beyond the four walls of the chapter house. As a growing number of colleges distance themselves from the so-called Greek system, Stephanie d'Arc Taylor considers the role of ritual in shaping this strained American institution.

The video opens on three young women standing at the front door of a large, stately house. They are dressed in uniform, their hair shimmering through the haze of a South Texas August. They give rehearsed speeches to convey welcome. Brilliant smiles gleam below inscrutable eyes. Then they open the doors, and the levees break. Dozens of identical sets of manicured hands and heads appear, grinning identical grins that border on the maniacal. A sea of young white women with glistening hair and teeth. The heads and hands move rhythmically, in unison, as if marshaled by an unseen drum major. They are yelling "woo."

The effect is unsettling and ponderous, like a postcard from Baudrillard's desert of the real. You feel the impulse to close the browser, to stand up, take a minute to process what you've seen. But when the video ends, the player automatically loads another video, with similar identical floating heads, clapping in time and baring perfect white teeth. There are thousands of them.

This is a door stack, a time-honored ritual practiced by American sororities to attract potential new members to join the organization. "It's something you'll typically see in the South, like Alabama, Ole Miss, Georgia," explains Lexi Solomon, an active member of the Kappa Kappa Gamma sorority at Virginia Tech. "We don't do door stacking, but we begin learning the songs for recruitment a couple months in advance. The week before recruitment we spend between five and nine hours per day practicing. But there's a lot I can't tell you because it's ritual."

The casual onlooker would be forgiven for describing the door stack as vaguely ridiculous. But Greek life—the collective term for American fraternities and sororities—is serious. Since the first fraternity was founded in the US—the Phi Beta Kappa Society, in 1776—it has become a keystone institution of the American economy, government and high society. Eighteen US presidents were fraternity brothers, as well as innumerable titans of every industry imaginable.

In America, a country without ancient aristocratic networks or economic guilds, fraternities create the types of shared backgrounds that mutually benefit members as they proceed through their careers. In the US as in Europe, vast riches and immense reserves of power have been created on the backs of these networks. And ritual is the major—in some cases, the only—thing that binds the albeit already very similar members of these organizations. (Until the 1960s, white fraternities and sororities were officially segregated. Today, there are several exclusively Black fraternities and sororities; the rest remain overwhelmingly white.)

But these rituals aren't just effusive performances by young women wearing pastel polo shirts screen-printed with Greek letters in metallic foil.

The initiation rituals, a closely guarded secret, carry "an air of gravitas," says Neil Duprey, a Sigma Alpha Epsilon alumnus of the University of California, San Diego. Duprey was raised in a nonreligious household, but says, "I've gone to church a few times with friends of various denominations. The SAE initiation rituals had a bit of that flair."

The religious undertones to Greek initiation rituals are no accident, says photographer Andrew Moisey. Moisey's 2018 book, *The American Fraternity*, is the result of seven years he spent shadowing a fraternity at the University of California, Berkeley. At one point, he found a 50-year-old ritual manual in an abandoned fraternity house. "The rituals were quasi-Christian, [positioning] brotherly spirit as the thing that separates fraternity brothers from the rest of society but also binds them to a higher calling," says Moisey.

In the ritual that initiates new members into the fraternity, according to Moisey's manual, young men go through a sort of resurrection. "You 'die,' are put into a coffin, and then you're reborn as a member of the brotherhood. That's also the ritual that Freemasons do, as well as born-again Christians," says Moisey.

Like Lexi Solomon, Duprey declined to give details of his chapter's rituals, as per fraternity policy. But his experience with initiation corroborates at least one aspect of Moisey's account: Sigma Alpha Epsilon "rents out the Masonic center in La Jolla [an affluent suburb of San Diego] as the setting," he says.

Greek life rituals can be useful for young men and women learning how to operate in the world. For Solomon, the process of joining a sorority showed her that she could handle situations in which she was under extreme scrutiny. "At the beginning, I was so nervous I was shaking like a Chihuahua," she laughs. But "going through the stress of recruitment and coming out the other side showed me that I could withstand a lot more than I thought I could. Social pressure was not something I was adept with, so it was a personal victory." The rituals represent a continuity she finds comforting. "For me, the rituals are about connecting with your sisters, the values that are important to you, and the history of the women who co-founded this organization."

For Duprey, the process of fraternity recruitment prepared him for job interviews, down to the business casual khakis-and-shirt dress code required for later-stage recruitment events. "It was an early introduction to the ways I would be interviewed at companies I was attempting to get jobs at. I just learned to talk about myself," he says.

Prior to initiation, prospective members of both sororities and fraternities traditionally undergo a period known as pledging. Horror stories about fraternity hazing abound, involving brothers forcing pledges to drink to excess, expose themselves to extreme weather conditions and consume spoiled food or even excrement. Neither Solomon nor Duprey report hazing that was scary or dangerous. But the figures speak for themselves: There was at least one hazing death per year at American universities from 1959 to 2019. Between 2005 and 2013 alone there were 60 deaths. The predominant cause of death is alcohol poisoning.

Fatal hazing rituals, as well as increased scrutiny on biased recruitment practices, have led many schools to crack down on Greek life on campus in recent years. Cornell, where Andrew Moisey teaches, is one of these. But he reports that fraternity alumni networks have pushed back against university sanctioning of fraternities, even in the wake of student deaths. Wealthy donors have threatened to withdraw contributions and even, in the case of Harvard, filed a civil rights suit against the university. In June, Harvard was compelled to remove a ban on Greek organizations on campus, on the grounds that the ban itself was discriminatory.

But growing grassroots opposition to Greek life is becoming harder to ignore. In the wake of George Floyd's killing in May 2020, a number of students at Southern universities typically regarded as Greek strongholds have joined the Abolish Greek Life movement, citing discriminatory recruitment practices and overtly racist histories. At Vanderbilt, outside Nashville, a third of Delta Tau Delta members have disaffiliated.

"At the beginning, I was so nervous I was shaking like a Chihuahua."

A representative of Kappa Kappa Gamma, Lexi Solomon's sorority, says that "a majority of our women at Vanderbilt University" remain members. Solomon, who is Cuban American, harbors no illusions about the past—or about the future of Greek life on American campuses. "There's a pretty racist history to Greek organizations," Solomon says plainly. "I know other schools are trying to abolish Greek life. Lately, we've been having difficult conversations about how we can be more accountable and do better for sisters of color and be more welcoming to people of color.... If a chapter is not doing that it's time to say goodbye."

But there have been efforts to reform fraternities and sororities for over a century. In 1873, Cornell banned secret societies after the death of Mortimer Leggett, who fell off a cliff to his death while being initiated into the Kappa Alpha Society. Today, one-third of Cornell undergraduates participate in Greek life. In October last year, the body of 18-year-old Cornell student Antonio Tsialas was found after a reportedly liquor-soaked fraternity hazing event.

Each new outrage—whether a hazing death or video of a sorority sister using a racial slur—spurs a round of performative pledges from Greek organizations to do better. For Moisey, this kind of lip service is representative of not only Greek life, but also the American institutions that its members eventually come to lead. "It's uniquely American," says Moisey. "Pledging to stand up to the highest ideals and then doing whatever they want. There's a close analogy between this behavior and the behavior the US has exhibited on the world stage. The place they learned this was in college."

NEW RITUALS

138

Ritual Design Lab suggests new rituals to mark the petty losses and small triumphs that pass without ceremony. Photography by Aaron Tilley & Set Design by Sandy Suffield

PREVIOUS: A RITUAL FOR A NEW HAIRCUT

Intention: To freshen, clean and protect your hair as it goes through a transition. *Props:* Olive oil, herbs, lemon. *Ritual flow:* 1. The morning before your haircut, get ready to take your last shower with your current hair style. 2. Before you do, take a small bowl of olive oil and mix in your favorite herbs—basil, mint, rosemary, sage or parsley. 3. Pour the oil and herbs over your head. Massage them into your hair. This is your protection mask before your cut. 4. After 20 minutes, take your shower and wash your hair. 5. Go to your haircut appointment. 6. When you come home, cut a lemon in half. 7. Squeeze it over your hair. This is the refresh.

A RITUAL FOR AIR TRAVEL

Intention: To make resolutions when you are in the liminal space of the airborne. *Prop:* Inflatable travel pillow. *Ritual flow:* 1. Buy an inflatable travel pillow before your flight and keep it in your carry-on bag. 2. When you are in the air, reflect back on what to keep in your life and what to let go. 3. Take a peek out the window and pick two or three clouds and whisper your resolutions (less caffeine in the afternoon, sign up for that Pilates class) to each of them. 4. When you are about to take a nap, pick up your pillow and blow each resolution inside while you are inflating it. 5. Enjoy your nap while your resolutions brew inside your pillow. 6. When you land, deflate the pillow. This officially lets the resolution spirits start their new life.

A RITUAL FOR DEATH WHEN YOU CAN'T ATTEND THE FUNERAL

Intention: To remember the person and preserve your memories. *Props:* Origami paper, a needle and thread. *Ritual flow:* 1. At the time of the funeral, sit down with some squares of paper and a pen. 2. Write down five memories that you have of the person who has died, each on a different square of paper. 3. For each memory, choose which origami form it should take: A crane, a boat, a flower, or something else that was meaningful to you and your lost one. 4. Thread a needle and push it through the origami pieces one at a time. 5. Hang the garland somewhere special.

A RITUAL FOR DECLUTTERING

Intention: To say goodbye to the things you have lived with, but are now giving away. Props: Soft brush, box, cologne, thank-you note. Ritual flow: 1. Pile up all the things you're planning on giving away. 2. One at a time, pick up each item. 3. Brush it off with three strokes. 4. Say thank you and goodbye. 5. Pack it carefully into the box. 6. Spray your cologne once onto it. 7. Wrap the box like a gift and include a thank-you note to the thrift store associate who is going to unbox it.

A RITUAL FOR A DEAD HOUSEPLANT

Intention: To show care and love to a plant that you might have neglected. *Props:* White cotton cloth, compost, water. *Ritual flow:* 1. Take your dead potted plant to a workspace outside. 2. Lay down a white cotton cloth. (You can use part of an old sheet or pillowcase.) 3. Gently remove the plant from its pot. 4. Shake loose the excess soil back into the pot. Use your fingers to clean the roots, like you are brushing someone's hair. 5. Lay the plant down on the cloth. 6. Fold the cloth over and around the plant, tucking the edges in. 7. Bury the wrapped plant in your garden, and cover it in compost. 8. Pour water over the burial site, and say goodbye.

A RITUAL FOR A LOST HANDBAG

Intention: To send prayers for the lost handbag to be found. *Props:* Post-it notes, glass jar, body of water. *Ritual flow:* 1. List all the items that got lost in the handbag, including the handbag itself. 2. For each lost item, pick a Post-it note, and write its name and a "Find your way back" wish. 3. Put all the Post-it notes into a jar that has a cap. 4. Write your home address on another Post-it note and add that to the jar as well. 5. Blow a wish inside the jar: "Come back with ease and grit!" Close the cap. 6. Submerge the jar in the closest river, creek, sea or lake. 7. Let each of your lost objects meet their spirits in the jar and find their way back home.

Death doula *Alua Arthur* talks to *Kyla Marshell* about preparing for life's final ritual. Photography by *Kanya Iwana*

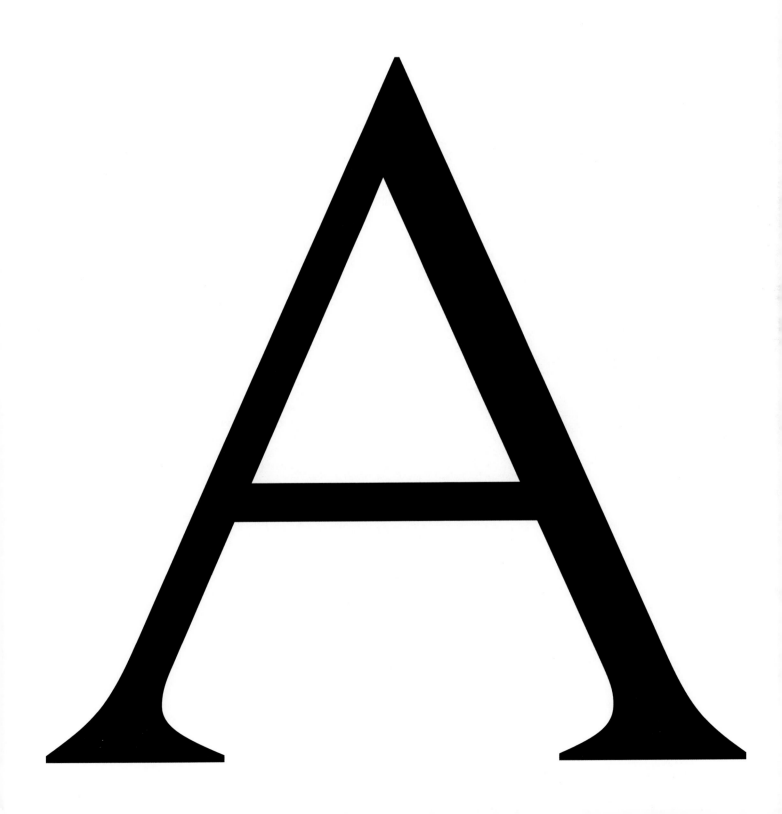

The most interesting version of the story is also the true one. This is how Alua Arthur reflects on the life-altering series of events that led her to become a death doula. She was burned out in her career as a lawyer in Los Angeles and so took a trip to Cuba as respite. On an errand one day, she narrowly missed getting hit by a car; then, later the same day, she found herself deep in conversation on a bus with a fellow passenger, a woman with cancer and who, it turned out, had been in the car that had almost hit her earlier. When, only a few months later, Arthur's brother-in-law got sick and eventually died, she became the support system for her sister, both in logistics and emotions. It was a process she had to learn in the midst of grieving for him herself. "I remember just sitting there and being like, Why isn't there somebody who already knows the answer? I would pay them anything," she says.

A year later, Going with Grace was born. Arthur's company offers not only services for the dying and their loved ones, but also training courses for those seeking to become death doulas, or who want to learn how to "be with dying." "We learn how people come into this world, but we don't learn how people go out," she says. "Most of us will be at the bedside of somebody we love who's dying. We should all get this training."

KM: *What were your ideas about death growing up? Was it something that you always felt comfortable with?* AA: I had to learn how to befriend it. I hadn't had any major impactful deaths before my brother-in-law. Then the woman on the bus [in Cuba]—she was only two years older than I was. I was like, Wow, we're all gonna die. I had to really start to get comfortable with the idea. It was useful for me, though, because I was depressed at the time. And so I used the opportunity to look at my life. Like, if this disease kills me—because let's make no bones about it, depression can be a terminal illness when left untreated—what have I done with my life, what have I made of my life, what do I value? What did I come to do? It was looking at those big questions through the lens of death as a way to help me understand my illness and ultimately as a way out of illness.

KM: *In one of your videos, you say that talking about death makes you feel more alive. What do you mean by that?* AA: Looking at a body that life has just left, you see the incredible stillness of it with the understanding that that person will not speak any more words. They'll never touch somebody again. They'll never get to look at their niece or listen to her laugh. They won't eat another orange. When I'm in my own life, doing those things, I bring so much more presence to it and a lot more gratitude. It's very life-affirming. Because I think, Ah, I'm actually still living. It also is a nice reminder that we don't know how much time we have left. So it's like, I'm here now. Let me do it now. Let me break up with that guy. Let me go to Fiji.

KM: *What would you like your own death to be like?* AA: I would

"Doula" is a word derived from a Greek term meaning "women who serve." Arthur says her services as a death doula extend from young people to whole families to even her own father.

"We learn how people come into this world, but we don't learn how people go out."

"*Talking about your death won't make it come—it's already coming.*"

like to be elderly, not too old. I still want to be able to enjoy moving around and being able to engage with living. I'd love to be in my own bed, hopefully on a deck someplace, in the house that I've owned and lived in for a while. I want to be outside, for sure. I'd like it to be around dusk. I want my family members to be around, but I don't want anybody to touch me, because I think that might ground me in earth and I want to feel free to fly. I want to smell some frankincense. I want to hear water trickling somewhere—just trickles, though, not a rush. I want to look at the colors in the sky and appreciate them one last time. I want to be able to look in the faces of the people that I loved, having already told them how much they mean to me and how full they've made my life; that loving them has been the greatest part of living in relationship with them. And then as soon as I die, or when it looks like I'm not going to breathe again, I want them to clap.

KM: *How young is too young to have a death plan? In an ideal society, would everyone have an end-of-life plan regardless of their age?* **AA:** Yes. Up until 18, parents are large-

ly responsible for decision-making. So after that point, particularly as kids are going away to college or starting to set up their own life and their own accounts [they should have one]. It's also, I think, important to instill in adolescents this idea of death and dying. Not that it's gonna stop them from making stupid choices, but maybe it'll make them more thoughtful.

KM: *How should the average person go about getting a death education?* **AA:** People can start simply by doing their own end-of-life planning. That'll start teaching them about some of the things that it takes. It's really important to spend some time thinking about who would make your decisions for you. What are your thoughts on life support? I think the pandemic really helped people start thinking about that because there's all this talk about ventilators. Think about what you want done with your body. What kind of [funeral] services do you want? Just give any direction, because even saying you want sunflowers as opposed to peonies can create a theme for a service. Get clear on who should take care of your pets. Do you have

a will, do you have a trust? Where are they? Because people hide those things away and nobody ever knows. All your finances—who's on your bank accounts, where are your retirement accounts, do you have life insurance? What are your passwords to your cellphone, to your computer, all your online banking, email passwords? Start to put some of that stuff down on paper and you'll get yourself a bit of a death education doing that.

If you don't do anything, the people who love you the most—the people that are going to be hardest hit by your death—are going to have to make decisions and try to figure out what you might want. [Not doing anything] is a self-centered approach, which we struggle with as a culture as a whole. We look so much at the independent person rather than thinking about the fact that we live in community. We're going to die in community, and that community is going to be responsible for wrapping up your life when you're not here anymore.

Try to think of it this way: Talking about your death won't make it come—it's already coming. It just makes you prepared for when it does.

Although based in Los Angeles, Arthur has started to train death doulas across the world through an online training forum, as well as offer her services through virtual consultation.

In her series Shedding Skin, photographer Yumna Al-Arashi offers an intimate insight into communal hammam traditions.

The hammam is perhaps the oldest surviving bathing ritual in the world. In many majority-Muslim countries, it remains an essential social space. Al-Arashi conceived of her hammam series while on an assignment in Tunis, but ended up shooting the final images with women in Beirut.

Al-Arashi, who was born in the US to a Yemeni father
and Egyptian mother, wanted to show the hammam as a healing and judgment-free space, counteracting its eroticized image in the West

Essay:
On Witchcraft

An interest in the occult has always coincided with times of institutional repression. With women, minorities and the environment all under direct threat from earthbound powers, it's no wonder a new generation of "baby witches" is finding strength in the supernatural. Words by *Rebecca Liu* & Collages by *Ignacio Cobo*

RITUALS

Among the many convulsions of the past few years—the rise of far-right ultranationalism, the roiling climate crisis, ever frenzied debates about the culture wars—there's been a more soothing, mystical countercurrent that harkens back to an older time: the explosive popularity of witchcraft, and all kinds of interest in the occult. Observing the sudden increase in books being published about witchcraft, including short story collection *Hex Life* and *Bitchcraft: Simple Spells for Everyday Annoyances & Sweet Revenge*, *The New York Times* asked last October if we had reached "peak witch."

The beloved '90s classic, *Sabrina the Teenage Witch*, was rebooted in a more stylish, spookier Netflix adaptation in 2018; the streaming platform also premiered *Siempre Bruja (Always a Witch)* the following year. And *Suspiria* and *The Witch* have returned witch stories to movie theaters. This summer, controversy erupted across social media when a group of TikTok "baby witches"—a term that refers to beginner practitioners who have yet to finesse their craft—were rumored to have tried to hex the moon; a severe transgression against witchcraft and nature. The incident introduced the term "WitchTok" into the broader cultural lexicon.

Over the past decade, many countries have seen a rise in witchcraft practitioners, whose beliefs range widely from a faith in the divinity of nature, to believing that the future can be shaped or changed through spellcraft and divination, to using ritual to connect with deities and ancestors—and much more. In 2014, a Pew Research Center study found that up to 1.15 million people identified as Wicca or Pagan in America, a 69% increase from previous figures in 2008. In the UK, *The Times* reported that "the growing popularity of modern versions of paganism, particularly among the young, has led the University of Edinburgh to appoint its first pagan honorary chaplain." Crucially, not all witches identify as Pagan or Wiccan (Pagan refers to a diverse assemblage of spiritual traditions including Druidry, Shamanism and Wicca). Many witches of color in the West practice witchcraft as a way of getting closer to their ancestors from regions including the Caribbean, Latin America and West Africa.

Younger generations, who take more fluid approaches to their practice, can often be found online. On TikTok, videos tagged #witchtok have amassed over 2 billion views. You can watch videos where witches, many of them young, release viewers of their curses or bad luck using incense sticks, perform tarot card readings or joke about dealing with criticism from Christian relatives. Though these online witchcraft communities often employ a tongue-in-cheek, surreal manner that is common in many internet subcultures, respect for shared traditions still stands—the baby witches who attempted to hex the moon were roundly condemned by their fellow witchtok-ers. Owen Davies, a historian of witchcraft and contemporary magic at the University of Hertfordshire, tells me, "In recent decades the concept of the modern witch has become much more democratic and diffuse, and hence more popular," pointing

In 1968, a women's protest group called W.I.T.C.H. staged a Halloween "hex" on Wall Street. Dressed in all black, with long peaked hats, the women squeezed glue into the door latches of financial institutions. The next morning, the bankers couldn't get in—and the Dow reportedly fell 13 points.

> *"Often when traditional institutions and beliefs collapse and people are caught between cultural despair and cosmic hopes, they turn to magic."*

to how television shows like *Charmed, Sabrina* and *Buffy the Vampire Slayer* "excited a teenage generation that they could accrue powers without having to be constrained by adherence to groups and set rituals."

For writer Rebecca Tamás, author of the poetry collection *WITCH*, published by Penned in the Margins in 2019, witchcraft in the modern world can offer "a push back against a rigid, Enlightenment rationality that has gone too far." She is referring to the 18th-century European movement that celebrated the primacy of reason over emotion, and the scientifically verifiable over the mystic. "This isn't hippy-dippy stuff," she explains, but rather an urgent call to see how "emotion, bodily experience and the spirit all have roles to play in shaping a harmonious world." It's unsurprising, with all that is going on in the world—Tamás lists "gender inequality, racial and sexual inequality, environmental crisis and rampant capitalism"—that witchcraft is having a resurgence.

Historians have traced how New Age interest in astrology flourished in the 1960s and '70s in America, then beset by political crises including the Vietnam War abroad, and protests and political crises domestically. In 1967, a 55,000-strong group of anti-war protestors marched to the Pentagon, and a group of radical activists known as the "yippies" tried to exorcise and levitate the headquarters of the Department of Defense. (Though it did not float, the poet Allen Ginsberg, who was at the scene, wrote, "The Pentagon was symbolically levitated in people's minds in the sense that it lost its authority which had been unquestioned

and unchallenged until then.") Writing in *The New York Times*, the author Michelle Goldberg remarked both of our current moment and of our history: "Often when traditional institutions and beliefs collapse and people are caught between cultural despair and cosmic hopes, they turn to magic."

It's unsurprising, then, that the resurgence of witchcraft in America has occurred alongside Donald Trump's presidency. Since his election, groups of witches across the country have cast spells against the president, with the help of candles, tarot cards, ashtrays and unflattering photos of Trump. Pop star Lana Del Rey has even joined in, imploring her fans on Twitter to gather ingredients for hexes. Trump, meanwhile, has made "witch hunt" one of his trademark slogans on Twitter, using it most recently to describe the multiple investigations into links between Russia and his 2016 campaign. On her campaign trail, Hillary Clinton was denounced by Trump's allies as a witch; others linked Clinton to Lucifer. Similar accusations have been leveled at Alexandria Ocasio-Cortez and Nancy Pelosi.

The 15th-century witch-hunting manual *Malleus Maleficarum* (The Hammer of the Witches) is widely seen to be the cause for the many trials and executions of witches across Europe and North America between the 15th and 19th centuries. It contended that while educated males dabbled in "learned" magic, it is women—with alleged lack of intelligence and susceptibility to "passions"—who were more likely to succumb to

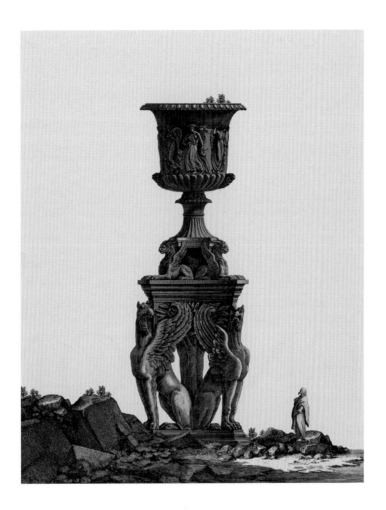

the Devil and thus transform into dangerous witches. To accusers, a witch seems to be any woman who steps beyond the narrow confines of what they deem acceptable femininity. Tamás explains, "The witch is a feminist figure because she resists any idea of 'ladylike' passivity and muteness—she takes what she wants, she's full of power and strength."

Davies notes that when laws against witchcraft were instituted across Europe in the 16th century, persistent fear of the Devil (and the women susceptible to him) meant that "there was a ready supply of suspects to report to the authorities." Today, people of all genders engaged in witchcraft still face this enduring suspicion, sometimes with fatal consequences; thousands of alleged witches across the world are killed each year. Suspicions of witchcraft led to deaths of the accused this summer in India, Ghana and South Africa.

But the internet and social media in the West have offered witches supportive communities in which to develop and explore. They also present more accessible—as well as just *more*—faces to witchcraft beyond the cauldron, pointy hat and the curse (though it can be that, too). London-based photographer Nicolette Clara Iles has been practicing for six years, and their work focuses on divination and tarot. "I see magic as a way through, a door into the known and unknown aspects of life, collective and self," they say. "In other ways, it's a returning to ancestral realization or wisdom." Iles's practice involves more than just ritual; it also shapes an orientation toward the world. By embracing the smallness of the rational, bounded self, the practice allows for a different way of being anchored in traditions and movements larger than oneself.

There are still many conversations to be had within the witch world. Iles notes that "There's been for a long time this idea of 'good magic' or 'white magic' and 'black magic.'" It's a division they deem "inherently racist, non-understanding and rooted in not only ignorance but even further colonial white supremacy." Many of the West's beloved witches of pop culture—Sabrina, the sisters of *Charmed*, Samantha from *Bewitched*—are white, traditionally beautiful and non-threatening, which is a far cry from the radical, dangerous and often racialized figure that witches sparked in imaginations centuries earlier. There are still so many more stories to tell. And as it rises in popularity, the co-option and commercialization of witchcraft grow with it: in 2018, the beauty chain Sephora pulled a "Starter Witch Kit" (sale price: $42) after backlash from witches.

But for practitioners themselves, their interest in witchcraft has little to do with the glamour or approval that comes from the commercial mainstream: It's rather about the discoveries they can constantly make on their own. Though it can be tempting to see the leap into the occult as a retreat—a search for safety and meaning in an increasingly difficult world—witchcraft also feels like an endlessly creative process that opens up more avenues for interrogation and revelation. "You never stop learning," Iles says of their practice: "Magic can be a way to navigate the world."

FIVE TIPS:

I SET INTENTION II

~~FOREVER FRIENDS~~

III

SHOW RESPECT IV

~~GO ONLINE~~

V MOVE ON

PHOTO
GRAPHY BY
GUSTAV
ALMESTÅL
&
STYLING BY
ANDREAS
FRIENHOLT

Set Intention

The distinction between a "ritual" and a "routine" can oftentimes be blurred, given that both types of action share the descriptive commonality of regularity. Does a ritual have to include traces of spirituality or elements of one's own cultural lineage? Can the same action be a ritual one day, and a routine the next?

It's easy to put our noses up at what other people call their "personal rituals," particularly on social media where people seem to be seeking outward validation for what you might logically imagine to be their most private habits. But Karen's mug of coffee with a splash of hazelnut creamer on the porch every Sunday could be a ritual *just as much* as Celeste's daily three-card tarot pulls and monthly brew of herbal medicine, passed down to her from her grandmother. There is no set-in-stone list of ritual actions; what distinguishes them from routine is intentionality.

Routine, we can safely say, is about self-discipline and the cultivation of self-integrity; it's a culmination of consciously chosen habits that show you that you *can*, after all, make promises to yourself that you keep. If you've read any self-help articles, you'll know that this repeated action over time will improve your life and well-being in a practical, measureable way.

Rituals are like routines that have been anointed with special powers only you are able to give them. They are ceremonial practices that signify something greater than the tangible sum of their parts. Collectively, we have tens of thousands of years of ancestral rituals vibrating in our epigenetics. Reclaiming your ritual rites can feel like a kind of homecoming. That's not to say that routines are devoid of this—they are just not fully quite *there* yet. Something may start out as a routine, and then transform into a ritual as it gets woven into the fabric of your life.

May we all live in a world where routines and rituals are cyclical and spiral in a dance of evolution and introspection. Any repeated action is inevitably going to seem dull, so why not *feel* differently about it and open up new realms of possibility in the sacred mundane?

Forever Friends

Even before you-know-what began, making arrangements with friends often felt needlessly tricky. Diary clashes, commutes, and work (or else lying supine and *recovering* from work) diminished occasions for quality time. To a certain extent, this is a hard-to-avoid part of growing up: In a 2016 study, researchers at Aalto University and the University of Oxford found that after the age of 25, we begin shedding casual friends to focus on closer ties. But that doesn't lessen the need to show up for the people who still matter. Many of us look back on the friendships we had in younger years as particularly strong. Childhood rituals like made-up languages, friendship bracelets or secret codes may seem goofy, but they formalize common bonds in an explicit way. Friendships in adulthood can be hazier—it's not always so easy to know if someone sees you as a close friend or as a casual pal to see once in a blue moon. But you can commit to spending more time with people you like without the need for matching necklaces. What about those mundane but important friendship routines from childhood, like taking the bus home together or movie marathons? Repeated ritual was what made childhood bonds so special, and it's just as good a way to strengthen your friendships today.

In her memoir *The Odd Woman and The City*, writer Vivian Gornick chronicles the simple arrangement she and her best friend, Leonard, have finessed over two decades: a walk, dinner and a movie. "Ours is the most satisfying conversation either of us has, and we can't bear to give it up even for one week," she writes. Having a long-standing commitment means you don't have to worry about planning something. Whether it's a phone call, drinks or shooting hoops at your neighborhood basketball court, knowing that say, Wednesday, 6 p.m., is your unmissable appointment together saves a lot of hassle.

Julie Beck, family editor at *The Atlantic*, knows all about the arrangements friends keep to stay close. In writing her column, *The Friendship Files*, she's learned that rituals are key for friendship in the long run: "It doesn't seem to matter what the ritual is—it's more that it gives them a reason to regularly come together," Beck explains over email. She's spoken to friends who have running clubs or coordinate annual vacations, middle schoolers who conduct "PowerPoint parties," and neighbors in New York who always look forward to sharing their subscription to *People*. "It's easy to put off catching up with a friend, or planning a hangout, so building in a routine makes that easier," she concludes. Beck loved the PowerPoint party concept—presenting subjects of interest to each other—so much that she's started one with her long-distance friends; so ask around—you may be surprised by how many offbeat ways there are to stay close.

Show Respect

Every August, I break wooden chopsticks into sections and insert them into an eggplant and a cucumber, four each. I fold bright strips of paper into zigzags and attach them to twisted rice straw rope, arranged alongside young bamboo fronds. We place nashi pears on the altar and light incense, then ring a bronze bell.

The cucumber is a horse, to convey my ancestors safely and swiftly here from the other world. And the eggplant is a cow, to carry them back slowly after their visit is over, because we wish they could linger. During this time of year, Obon, the boundary between this world and the next is easily permeable, and by performing these rites, by chanting and praying and completing actions in a preordained order, we are easing the spirits' transition. As I go through the steps, senses are engaged, memories flood. I feel myself closer to my predecessors.

To the outsider, though, this Buddhist-Confucian custom may look ridiculous: a bunch of twists of paper and some vegetables with sticks in them.

Ridiculous is relative. Some of us leave our teeth under our pillows in hopes that a fairy might visit in the night to buy them. Or hang socks on the wall and put out cookies in hopes that a fat man flying across the sky with a herd of reindeer might come and fill the socks with gifts. Or step on a glass at a wedding, dip a baby in a river, wind ribbons around a pole while wearing a flower crown.

A ritual at its best helps us to access deeper meaning. The intricate steps can feel like a magic spell to unlock some mystery of life. For many, rituals are deeply personal, contemplative and sacred. They wear grooves in a culture, carved from the weight of history. In fol-lowing those well-worn tracks, we travel the road our forebears laid, evoking a cellular familiarity.

What about when those rituals are only skin-deep, and you're an outsider looking in? A lot has been said about cultural appropriation versus appreciation. At its core, the difference is about power and respect. A quick survey of keywords like "rituals and traditions around the world" on the internet yields scores of facile clickbait articles meant to shock and titillate, using words like "craziest," "weird" and "bizarre." It's no wonder people feel protective and affront-ed. When our dearest traditions are reduced to a quickie Insta-gram post, or are commodified for cash, it stings.

It doesn't have to be that way. People are often eager to share their beloved customs with receptive new friends. As teenagers renting a little flat in Andalusia, my friend and I invited most of the neighborhood to our table for a Thanksgiving meal. Even though that particular holiday doesn't ex-ist in Spain, our guests could eas-ily appreciate gratefulness, con-viviality and food. And in return, they gave us red underwear on New Year's Eve.

Rituals deepen connection, and cultural exchange is inevi-table. When studying the mean-ings behind the rites we perform, we often find there's more to con-nect us than we thought. We use them to celebrate love, remember the dead, mark momentous occa-sions. When done with invitation, listening and reciprocity, it can be an experience tinged with warmth and camaraderie.

At the end of three days, we point the horse and the cow west-ward, and light another stick of agarwood. "Safe journey," we tell them. "See you next year."

Go Online

In 2020, many social rituals took place online or not at all. Zoom became a place for farewell drinks, graduations, anniversaries and even funerals. But digital conversations can feel stilted at the best of times, and even the loudest "Cheers" rings hollow in an empty room. Could it ever be otherwise? Kursat Ozenc, co-founder of the LA-based Ritual Design Lab, studies existing rituals, and designs new ones—including those on page 138. Here, he shares tips on translating physical rituals into the digital sphere.

BG: *Why do we have rituals?* **KO:** Rituals are the bedrock of our sense-making in this world. According to Nick Hobson and his colleagues at the University of Toronto, they help us regulate emotions, our goal/performance states, and our connection to other people. From the outside, rituals could look irrational or non-functional, because they do not make "logical" sense. But rituals tell a story that can help us make sense of something, and move past it.

BG: *How will rituals change when the physical elements can't happen, like during this pandemic?* **KO:** Ideally, rituals need to have a physical component. But if that isn't possible, people will find a workaround, like relying on certain senses more than others. For instance, video calls use vision, audio calls use hearing. Our rituals will be adapting to these audiovisual-heavy experiences.

BG: *How can we successfully translate real-world rituals into the digital sphere?* **KO:** People start with skeuomorphing [creating structures that mimic older ways of doing things] real-life rituals, and then experimenting with digital native ones. We practically live in a blend of the two. To be successful, someone creating a ritual should ask: What's my intention and purpose in this ritual? How can I embody that intention?

BG: *Which rituals work best when translated digitally?* **KO:** Social gatherings like birthday parties, happy hours—they're the trickier ones. Things get harder in digital when the occasion isn't goal-oriented. If there is a goal, like your weekly stand-up meeting at work, it's easier to establish a digital ritual, since you rely less on personal interactions and more on the content of the meeting.

BG: *What can we do to make online farewell drinks less awkward?* **KO:** Keep it short! Be inclusive—some people don't drink, maybe explicitly say it's okay to bring a soft drink. Find a moment when people can toast toward the camera. Perhaps use a fork to simulate the clinking sound.

BG: *How can you prepare your physical surroundings for a virtual gathering?* **KO:** Having a "less is more" approach will be helpful. Imagine viewers who are trying to process tens of backgrounds in gallery view. For a funeral, plants or calming scenery will be good. For a wedding, a background that warms up people can be good, maybe a memory or interest that you and the couple share together. If you know other people who are also invited you can create a background together, so it's more of a shared experience.

BG: *What's the best way of dealing with the lack of eye contact?* **KO:** Think of analog situations. If you are communicating audio-only, frame this as a radio play, where you are one of the actors. If there's video, frame it as a movie: It's 100% fine to feel like all eyes are on you, because you're the hero or heroine in the story.

Move On

Knowing when it's time to let go of a personal ritual can be a complicated process. The release of anything familiar is difficult, especially if it's a regular activity that has provided a comforting rhythm during uncertain times. But becoming self-aware (and self-inquisitive) about personal rituals can lead to fresh realizations.

"When we perform any kind of personal ritual, what we're doing is looking for something—maybe it's energy, or the feeling of being grounded and centered," says Natalia Rosenbaum, a holistic psychotherapist based in the Boston area. "So the first thing to ask yourself would be, Am I still getting anything out of this ritual? If you're not gaining what you need from it, then it's probably time to move on."

Likewise, it's important to notice if a ritual has become depleting. If accidentally forgetting the ritual or choosing not to do it leads to shame and self-criticism, these feelings can point to having created unhealthy attachments to the activity. "For example, if someone's morning ritual was to go for a run, but then it started to feel more like a burden that activated their guilty conscience if they didn't do it every day, that would be an indication to step back and change it up," Rosenbaum says. "Rituals are a way that we can create a sense of wholeness, peace and understanding. They help to bring us into a more integrated way of being. If that's not the case anymore, invite curiosity and self-compassion. Find what feels special and sacred to you."

For particularly sentimental rituals, letting go might feel more like a grieving process than a simple conscious adjustment. Oftentimes, these types of rituals are the ones that involve others: loved ones who have passed, ex-romantic partners, or family members who now live far away.

While heartache has its purpose in the healing process, repeating a ritual that brings up needless pain or longing could become a kind of emotional addiction. "The difference between a positive ritual and addictive behavior is that, with the latter, someone knows that they should probably stop, but they can't. We can be addicted to a certain feeling—it doesn't even have to be substance-induced," adds Rosenbaum. With heightened awareness, it's possible to shift into new ways of being and transmute old rituals that have lost their original purpose.

Relish the transformation of rituals, even if it means saying goodbye to one that has been a part of your life for a long time. The result will almost certainly be reflective of your growth—and self-awareness.

How to retire a ritual. Words by Alia Gilbert

4.

Directory

178 — 192

ANDREW DURBIN

Peer Review

Andrew Durbin, editor of *frieze* magazine, on the magnetic allure of writer and photographer *Hervé Guibert*.

Who first warned me about Hervé Guibert? It must have been a good friend, someone who knew what would happen to me when I read this French novelist and photographer, whose books offer such frank analyses of ambition, love, desire, sex, disease and decay. His essays on photography, collected in *Ghost Image* (1981), and his late autobiographical novels, like *To the Friend Who Did Not Save My Life* (1990), extend a firm grip once you find yourself within their reach, and never let you go.

Guibert portrays his experience as a gay man in Mitterand's France with an arresting, almost cinematic quality, developing characters in densely symbolic and richly layered narratives reminiscent of Alfred Hitchcock's *Vertigo* (1958). Like Hitchcock, Guibert masterfully weaves deception and revelation, death and resurrection in stories of lovers, family, his friends, his mentor Michel Foucault, and himself. Not always factual, necessarily, since he deliberately fudges events to construct a more compelling portrait of why we live the way we live, Guibert made of his circle a secular book of saints. (I wonder what he would think of such a metaphor; the religious power that lies under the surface of modernity never seemed to captivate him as it had Foucault.)

Guibert is impossible to put down. Each time I return to him I am on entirely new ground. Reading him, I find myself suspended, like Jimmy Stewart in *Vertigo*, between dream and reality, desire and horror. His description in *Ghost Image*, of a favorite Diane Arbus photograph summarizes the effect: "I found in this picture an emotion similar to madness, or happiness, I was never able to determine which, and it was this disturbance, something between horror and freedom, that fascinated me. Was I supposed to enjoy this image, and was my enjoyment legitimate?"

TO THE FRIEND WHO DID NOT SAVE MY LIFE

by Andrew Durbin

To the Friend Who Did Not Save My Life is Hervé Guibert's most famous book. Released in France in 1990, its publication caused a stir when it revealed, in a lightly fictionalized sequence, that Guibert's mentor, Michel Foucault (named Muzil in the book), had died from complications due to AIDS. Previously, the press had reported Foucault's death from cancer. Here, in 100 brief and brutal chapters, Guibert methodically dispenses with the fiction, as it were, by revealing the true cause and course of the philosopher's decline—which would soon be his own.

KATIE CALAUTTI

Object Matters

It's safe to presume that for as long as humans have existed, they've grappled with the inevitability of death. For much of that existence, they have found ways to immortalize the struggle via memento mori. Roughly translating from Latin as "Remember that you must die," memento mori are symbolic reminders of death in art, literature, philosophy, fashion, and architecture. The common symbols associated with them—skulls, fruit, flowers, snuffed candles, and clocks—serve to remind us that life is fleeting and fragile; they're the morbid yin to carpe diem's yang.

The phrase as a philosophy is believed to have taken root in ancient Roman times, when victorious generals paraded through the streets, followed closely by a slave who whispered continuous reminders of mortality to the worshipped war hero. As the Black Death swept through Europe in the 13th century and the Catholic church solidified its views on purgatory, a theological framing of memento mori was widely adapted. Christianity focused memento mori's appeal through a hyper-religious lens that boiled human existence down to a preparation for the afterlife.

With the opening up of global trade roots, there was a memento mori boom during the Middle Ages and Renaissance. From the 1500s to 1700s, artisan-made ivory prayer beads, sculptures, and other talismans depicting death and decay were coveted by wealthy collectors and royalty. Ironically, these items—meant to underscore the impermanence of status and wealth—were quite costly. Dutch artists in the veritas movement of the 17th century painted still lifes depicting hourglasses, destroyed books, wilted flowers, and rotting food to underscore the transient nature of earthly existence. And later, Victorian rings depicting skulls and skeletons were worn by everyone from the queen to her poorest subjects.

Today, memento mori are interwoven in the collective unconscious—from the skull iconography used by fashion brands to *Game of Thrones'* oft-quoted "Valar Morghulis" ("All men must die"). Our time may be limited, but the knowledge that death rules us all is immortal.

A macabre history of memento mori.

Peter Smisek wallows in the glory of the bathhouse.

Drink two to four glasses of cool water after each sauna; the average person will produce a pint of sweat during even a short session. *Photograph: Ruth Kaplan*

PETER SMISEK

Cult Rooms

Banya, sauna, hammam, bathhouse, spa, *sentō, jjimjilbang,* sweat lodge. Throughout much of the world, a weary traveler will sooner or later stumble upon some combination of water, steam and communal nudity. Used, in varying measure, for recreation, hygiene, spiritual enlightenment or social (and sometimes physical) intercourse, each one presents a distinct set of spaces, rules and rituals.

Some bathing cultures are a result of happy geomorphological accidents—think of Iceland's rugged thermal pools or the refined Japanese *onsen.* Some encourage indulgence, like the opulent spas of continental Europe; others, like the Finnish sauna or the Russian *banya,* foster a more egalitarian spirit. But there are cross-cultural commonalities among all that oscillate between hedonism and asceticism, between pleasure and virtue. Remote Russian villages and some private homes still feature traditional banyas, but they were gradually adapted to the more urbane ways of Russia's Europhile urban elite in the 17th century—and not without an illustrious precedent. "They also have roots in the bathing traditions of the ancient Romans, which made their way to what is Russia today via Byzantium," says Ethan Pollock, professor of His-

tory and Slavic Studies at Brown University and author of *Without the Banya, We Would Perish.* "The urban, public, communal banya that we see in Russian cities today often have features that are reminiscent of both the rural sweat lodge and the urban bathhouse."

In Russia's banyas, bathers still whip each other with bundles of birch branches before sprinkling cold water on hot stones to make steam. Temperatures inside can reach a sizzling 200 degrees Fahrenheit; once bathers have worked up a sweat, they take a dip in a cold plunge pool. Sexes aren't always segregated and the bathers are mostly nude.

In the early modern era that followed the Middle Ages, Western European observers came to think that bathhouses were backward and licentious. They were believed to be places of iniquity and contagion where sexes and classes mixed and socialized—practices that had been all but eradicated on the continent by the church. Moral panics would continue, of course. In the 1980s, as the AIDS epidemic tore through New York's queer community, the city's gay bathhouses were closed down after Dr. Yehudi M. Felman of New York City's Bureau of Venereal Disease Control speculated that the cause of the plague "could

be the bugs out of the pipes in the bathhouses." But bathhouses and bathing cultures the world over have proved remarkably resilient, despite the rise of indoor plumbing and private bathrooms threatening to supplant their hygienic function. In Finland, there is about one sauna for every two people living in the country, and there's a rising interest in the ancient tradition of smoke saunas. In Russia, the banya has survived revolutions, the planned economy, the breakup of the Soviet Union and the country's return to capitalism. Surely there must be something universal in the bathhouse's appeal. Could it be the potent mix of sweat, broken-down barriers and a commonly held sense of ritual?

According to Pollock, the bathhouse's resilience and appeal lie in its versatility. "It has a tendency to morph into a tradition that appears valuable for whatever zeitgeist exists at any given time in any given place," he says. Frequented by peasants and czars, students and retirees, artists and businesspeople, revolutionaries and reactionaries, for business or for leisure, the bathhouse is a place equally suited for silent meditation as it is for bacchanals. "If it had just been a place to get clean," Pollock concludes, "it would have died out."

KATIE CALAUTTI

Bad Idea: Gender Reveals

It's time to burst the (pink or blue) bubble of this trend.

What if you learned that a completely frivolous celebration you had planned could result in bodily injury, a massive explosion, a devastating fire or even death? Now add to it the fact that the guest of honor would be pregnant. Would you still host it? Based on the growing popularity of gender-reveal parties over the last decade, the answer for many is a resounding *yes*.

It all started innocently enough. In 2008, pregnant blogger Jenna Myers Karvunidis gathered her family to cut a cake: The pink-hued contents announced to all (Myers Karvunidis included) that her first baby was a girl. *The Bump* picked up the story, and a hot new trend was born—as well as her daughter Bianca.

Alongside the rise of social media (and concurrently, an almost Pavlovian obsession with going viral), excited parents-to-be dreamed up increasingly elaborate spectacles of one-upmanship. The conceit had all the makings of a schadenfreudian social experiment: a crowd of unsuspecting people, a surprise, a reaction, and—of course—cameras trained on everyone for the duration. And so, naturally, tragedy ensued.

There was the Louisiana man who fed a melon full of blue Jell-O to an alligator and almost lost a limb; the Arizona man who set off colorful fireworks and sparked a 47,000-acre wildfire; and the Iowa woman who was killed by shrapnel from a homemade device meant to reveal her grandchild's gender. Broken bones and burns have become an unsurprising side effect of these gatherings—and yet the trend has persisted.

Beyond the physical dangers, the concept of a gender reveal is both archaic and harmful. Gender is something a person defines for themselves, but these parties place an unborn child into a box, underscoring roles and expectations through assignment.

In July 2019, Myers Karvunidis revealed that Bianca now prefers to dress in gender-nonconforming suits. She expressed regret about the party that sparked it all, saying she's learned that focusing on gender is limiting to a child's potential. Perhaps the target of these reveals will be the ones to end them for good.

GOOD IDEA

by Harriet Fitch Little

Not all gender reveal parties are created equal. In 2017, Ohio couple Love and Brandon Gwaltney organized a reveal with a difference. "We wanted to announce that we got it wrong 17 years ago when we told the world we were having a little girl," Love wrote in a Facebook post that quickly went viral. "So, we'd like to introduce you to our son: Grey." In the accompanying images, Grey—who is nonbinary but uses male pronouns—emerges from a box of multicolored balloons. His mother, who is pregnant in the photos, apologizes to viewers who came to the post expecting to find out the gender of the couple's next child: "Sorry (not sorry) to disappoint you."

BELLA GLADMAN

Last Night

What did design dealer *Michael Bargo* do with his evening?

Michael Bargo knows the value of home. Renowned for his fashionable clientele (including Mary-Kate Olsen, co-creative director of The Row) and for his Instagram tastemaking, Bargo has filled his uptown New York apartment with design classics, which he sells to clients who come to visit.

BG: *What did you do last night?* **MB:** I went for dinner with a client at Raoul's, a classic SoHo restaurant that's been there for 40 years. I wouldn't have gone out if he hadn't been in town from LA! I'm a real homebody—unsurprising, for someone who works in interiors. **BG:** *Where's home?* **MB:** I've been slowly moving into this new place uptown since June. It has a doorman, and the architecture is a little *American Psycho*. I brought the most significant pieces of my collection, like my black Borsani sofa, and I've been experimenting with color; I now have a yellow rug and a blue Prouvé dining table!

BG: *What prompted your move?* **MB:** I used to have a gallery/apartment in Chinatown, but my lease was up. This new place is consider-ably smaller, but there's still room to entertain. I used to have dinner parties for 15 to 20 people—I've become close friends with most of my clients. Now it's six to eight maximum. Obviously big gatherings are out right now, but I've got company: my two cats and my Chihuahua mix, Timo. His back legs are paralyzed: When we go out, he scoots about on wheels.

BG: *Are you a good cook?* **MB:** Not at all, despite loving to host dinners. I like to do something simple yet extravagant, ordering sushi platters, or serving baked potatoes or spaghetti with caviar.

BG: *Do you worry that parties and pets are at odds with your pristine furniture?* **MB:** No. Although the French mid-century pieces I like and work with are considered masterpieces, they were made to be used in factories and public buildings. They can handle wear and tear! Take a piece by Charlotte Perriand/Le Corbusier; horsehair's much easier to clean than a linen sofa. Think about it: If you poured wine on an animal, it wouldn't stain!

Bargo's primary obsession is French mid-century furniture from designers such as Jean Prouvé and Charlotte Perriand.

Photograph: Valerie Chiang

Meet the classical composer whose unornamented arrangements fill arenas.

TOM FABER

Max Richter

For someone whose music has such a subtle, delicate fingerprint, Max Richter has had a seismic influence over the past decade in music. His signature sound rejects classical music's convoluted flourishes, focusing instead on emotive, accessible string and piano figures interwoven with electronic sounds. He influenced a whole school of composers, including Nils Frahm, Ólafur Arnalds and Jóhann Jóhannsson, to perform contemplative music to arena-sized crowds.

While he continues to refine his musical style, the German-born British composer, 54, ceaselessly seeks to meet his listeners in new spaces. He has composed for ballet, television (*Black Mirror*) and film (*Ad Astra, Arrival, Waltz with Bashir*). His ambitious 2015 project *Sleep* was an 8½-hour piece performed to audiences sleeping in museums. These formal experiments are underpinned by intellectual inquiries, like his new album, *Voices*, which incorporates readings from the 1948 Universal Declaration of Human Rights.

TF: *Your compositions have addressed the Iraq War, the 7/7 London bombings and Guantanamo Bay. Is your music always a response to something?* **MR:** If you're an artist, the work you make is your response to being alive, part of figuring out what it's all about. Creative works are spaces to think, where I ask "What if?" questions and the listener brings their biography to it. The musical work becomes a conversational space.

TF: *Is your music a conversation or a monologue? After all, you're expressing and the audience is listening.* **MR:** That's the magic of live performance—you hear back. You understand what you've made for the first time when people hear it. I've built a minimal musical language over the years in order to allow that conversational space. When I was trained as a composer, the orthodoxy was to write very complex music, impossible to play and impossible to listen to. That felt like an authoritarian position, so instead I took elements away from my work to open a space for the listener to inhabit without being lectured at.

TF: *What "space" did you want to create with* Sleep? **MR:** A *Sleep* performance is half-concert, half-gallery work, with people in hundreds of beds. The musicians accompany what's going on in the room, rather than projecting a text to a passive audience, so it overturns the power dynamics between performers and listeners.

TF: *Why do you so often place narrators in your work, ranging from Eleanor Roosevelt to Murakami to Kafka?* **MR:** It's about clarity, almost like a front door for the piece that listeners can walk through. In *Voices*, I wanted to use the Universal Declaration of Human Rights because I think it's the most astounding document, made more relevant since we're a long way from its goals and only getting further away.

TF: *In the press, your music is described with contrived genre tags like "neo-classical" and "post-minimal." What does "classical music" mean today?* **MR:** Classical music describes a culture rather than the musical material itself. It describes a set of social attitudes and rituals, which are actually problematic. People have to go to a concert hall, sit quietly, they're not allowed to clap. There are power structures implied by the old man standing at the front telling everyone what to do. This stops people from being able to simply encounter the sounds. Classical music, in its purest sense, is one of the greatest achievements of humanity. On another level, it's got a slightly oppressive, authoritarian aspect to it.

Starred clues will guide your crossword "ritual".

ANNA GUNDLACH

Crossword

ACROSS

1. Significant religious division
7. Snoop or Nate of hiphop
11. Card than can be high or low
14. "Right, that makes sense now!"
15. Ireland's best-selling solo artist
16. Chance to win an Oscar, for short
17. Playfully chomps on
18. Big name in luxury cars
19. Chewable stick
20. *People who let their self-importance get in the way of wedding rituals?
22. Supreme Court Justice Kagan
24. 2016 Olympics host
25. Shared by us
26. Letter-shaped bike locks
27. *Merit another oracle for the divination ritual?
30. Flooded
33. Wizened woman of folklore
34. Big hullabaloo
35. Deflation indication
38. Barking swimmer of the Pacific
41. Abbr. on a wanted poster
42. Choose
44. French sci-fi pioneer
45. *Rituals meant to summon the creator of "Hamilton"?
50. "Carmen" and "The Magic Flute"
51. Direction opposite WSW
52. Locale in a Beach Boys hit
55. Like hair first thing in the morning
56. *Mantras heard at the suet and lard ritual?
59. University's web ending
60. Adult material
62. Mazda alternatives
63. It means nothing
64. Word that might annoy a grammar prescriptivist
65. Indigenous
66. Skin pic
67. Ono who said "A dream you dream together is reality"
68. Rust and laughing gas

DOWN

1. Navigation aid for subs and bats
2. Dish whose spiciness can be measured in alarms
3. Aware of, in old slang
4. Rae of "Insecure"
5. Put a crust on, as a steak
6. Rock that might fall in a shower
7. Blondie vocalist Harry
8. Change for a five
9. OB/___
10. Garden party structure
11. Thin relative of spaghetti
12. Put trust in
13. Oscar winner for "La La Land"
21. Rev, as an engine
23. Cut branches from
26. Give a nudge to
27. Self starter?
28. Tuna in a poke bowl
29. Faux ___ (social blunder)
30. Instant where everything falls into place
31. Collaboratively written reference
32. Consequently
36. Silently approves
37. Student transcript stat
39. Many a well known NYC st.
40. Guitar innovator Paul
43. Pick up the tab for
46. ___ Technica (tech news website)
47. Be a real party pooper
48. Savings acct. accumulation
49. Electronic dance genre originating in 1980s Detroit
52. Pushed Ctrl-Z, maybe
53. Fend (off)
54. Beasts of burden
56. George Clinton's genre
57. Bamboozle
58. On the negative side
61. "O Sole ___"

DAPHNÉE DENIS

Correction

Don't be fooled by spurious data.

Legend has it that storks deliver babies, and there are numbers to prove it. In 2000, British mathematics professor Robert Matthews found a correlation between birth rates in 17 European countries and the number of storks nesting in them. Coincidence? Why, yes, of course. Matthews had set out to demonstrate to his students the perils of equating correlation and causation. Yet his findings could be misconstrued to argue, albeit somewhat unconvincingly, that there is only a one in 125 chance that storks do not, in fact, bring human babies into the world. The correlation between breeding storks and birth rates in Europe, he concluded, was "statistically significant, not immediately explicable and causally nonsensical."

It is easy to believe that when two variables follow the same trend, one must necessarily cause the other. Those looking for patterns in two datasets with a seemingly strong link to one another (say, a given diet and a given health effect) can be tempted to infer causality simply from observing variables moving together. And yet, as statistics students around the world have heard over and over again, correlation does not imply causation. A correlation could be random. The missing causal link between two trends could be a third variable altogether. There is simply no way of knowing without further investigation.

Statistically significant yet ridiculous correlations help bring the point home, as evidenced by the website and book *Spurious Correlations* by Harvard Law School graduate Tyler Vigen. In a series of both factual and absurd charts, he shows, for example, the little-known correlation between the per capita consumption of mozzarella cheese and the number of civil engineering doctorates awarded in the US. Or how a drop in margarine consumption matches a lower divorce rate in Maine. Data can be twisted to support weak arguments. Don't be fooled by correlations without a cause.

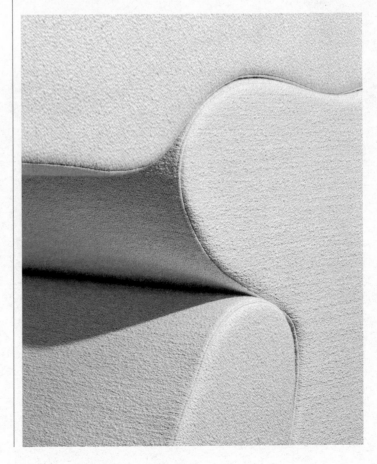

Spurious correlations are a potentially dangerous tool of disinformation. In 2007, a slight correlation was all it took for one Fox News pundit to suggest that universal health care contributed to a rise in terrorism.

HOUSE OF FINN JUHL

53 SOFA 1953
BY **FINN JUHL**

finnjuhl.com

Stockists

16ARLINGTON
16arlington.co.uk

A.W.A.K.E MODE
awake-mode.com

AHLUWALIA
ahluwaliastudio.com

BALENCIAGA
balenciaga.com

BALLY
bally.com

BODE
bodenewyork.com

BY FAR
byfar.com

CHALAYAN
chalayan.com

CHRISTIAN WIJNANTS
christianwijnants.com

CHRISTOPHER JOHN ROGERS
christopherjohnrogers.com

CHRISTOPHER KANE
christopherkane.com

COMPLETEDWORKS
completedworks.com

DRIES VAN NOTEN
driesvannoten.com

EDAS
edas.store

GREEN RIVER PROJECT
greenriverprojectllc.com

GUCCI
gucci.com

HANDVAERK
handvaerk.com

HERMÈS
hermes.com

HOUSE OF FINN JUHL
finnjuhl.com

ISSEY MIYAKE
isseymiyake.com

JOSEPH
joseph-fashion.com

KIMHÉKIM
kimhekim.com

LEJE
lejeofficial.com

LIVE THE PROCESS
livetheprocess.com

MARC JACOBS
marcjacobs.com

MARIA BLACK
maria-black.com

MIU MIU
miumiu.com

MM6 MAISON MARGIELA
maisonmargiela.com

PARACHUTE HOME
parachutehome.com

PORTUGUESE FLANNEL
portugueseflannel.com

PRADA
prada.com

REJINA PYO
rejinapyo.com

ROKSANDA
roksanda.com

ROLEX
rolex.com

SIMONE ROCHA
simonerocha.com

STRING
stringfurniture.com

SUN WOO
sunwoo-official.com

TCHAI KIM
tchaikim.co.kr

THE BREAK
shopthebreak.com

TINA FREY
tinafreydesigns.com

TOGA ARCHIVES
toga.jp

VAQUERA
vaquera.nyc

nature, delivered.

Genovese basil

PICCOLO

piccoloseeds.com | SEEDS FOR CONTEMPORARY GARDENS | ig @piccolo.seeds

Credits

COVER
Photographer
Giseok Cho
Stylist
Yeon You
Hair
Hyunwoo Lee
Makeup
Seongseok Oh
Model
Sungsik Min wearing a skirt
by Kimhekim

MIRANDA JULY
Photo Assistants
Fred Mitchell
Patrick Molina
Producers
Ben Bibriesca
Jeremy Thomas at
Hyperion LA

RINA SAWAYAMA
Photo Assistant
Cameron Williamson

UNDER THE ILLUSION
Photo Assistant
Benjamin Whitley
Styling Assistant
Sammiey Hughes
Casting
Sarah Bunter

NEEDLE WORK
Models
Miki Kim
Sungsik Min

ABBY STEIN
Set Design Assistant
Jeremy Gecker
Styling Assistant
Avery McQueen

NEW RITUALS
Photo Assistant
Lucas Aliaga-Hurt

Special Thanks
Annabel Cohen
Bo Kelly
Tal Janner-Klausner

JOHN CLIFFORD BURNS

My Favorite Thing

Death doula *Alua Arthur*, interviewed on page 148, tells the story behind her favorite crystal.

Regardless of whether you give credence to the power of crystals, you may already be using them in your beauty regimen. Crystal hair combs, facial rollers and *gua sha* tools for massage have become popular in recent years. As is the case with crystals in a more traditional form, the belief is that they promote healing energy.

This crystal belonged to my brother-in-law, Peter, who died from Burkitt's lymphoma in 2013. My sister wasn't yet ready to pack up all of his things or to get rid of them, so we just moved his belongings into storage briefly. About six months later, we went through them and I found a crystal at the bottom of a backpack that he'd probably used for traveling. Since I'm a traveler and have often traveled with only a backpack, I found it significant. I took the crystal and now I tuck it into my own backpack whenever I go traveling.

I was in Sri Lanka on the day that a park bench, which was dedicated to him, was unveiled. While I couldn't be with my family in New York for the unveiling of his bench, I put the crystal out on the windowsill all night long. I was able to feel like I was with him through his crystal. That's why I love it. It's not particularly unique or special; it's just that it belonged to a man that I loved dearly. It's the last little bit I have of him—other than his leather jacket, but don't tell my sister that.